dog
knows

Let's enable dogs
    & humans to
hold space for each other.

Sindhoor

dog knows

learning how
to learn from dogs

sindhoor
pangal

HarperCollins *Publishers* India

First published by HarperCollins *Publishers* in 2021
Building 10, Tower A, 4th Floor, DLF Cyber City, Phase II,
Gurugram Haryana – 122002, India
www.harpercollins.co.in

2 4 6 8 10 9 7 5 3 1

P-ISBN: 978-93-9016-385-4
E-ISBN: 978-93-9016-386-1

Typeset in 11.5/15.2 Adobe Garamond at
Manipal Technologies Limited, Manipal

Printed and bound at
MicroPrints India, New Delhi

Dedicated to my darling Nishi and Uttam,
my guiding lights, my inspiration and my strength

CONTENTS

Foreword by Turid Rugaas   ix

Preface   xi

1. We Become a Family   1

2. Early Education   39

3. The Boarding that Never Happened   74

4. The Cheerwal   106

5. Unlearning   143

6. The Lives of Streeties   181

7. Respecting the Mind   219

8. Beyond Behaviour   241

9. Talking to Animals   276

Acknowledgements   295

About the Author   298

FOREWORD

Dear Readers,
     As Sindhoor's friend, teacher and colleague, it was a pleasure for me to read the manuscript for her book when it first came to me. On the one hand, her personal story, coming from the heart, makes the book come alive and easy to relate to. On the other hand, Sindhoor's sound and wise advice, backed by her experience as a dog behaviour consultant, makes it valuable to anyone who wants to understand their dogs better. I have read all of Sindhoor's articles and columns, which have been interesting and well written, so I read this book with curiosity. And she did not disappoint!

Dog Knows: Learning How to Learn from Dogs is a warm and lovely addition to the world of dog books, with new and refreshing approaches to problems pet parents often come across in their daily lives with dogs. I have no doubt it will help many people and their dogs in achieving a better life together. The markedly different approach that

Sindhoor offers, compared to other dog books in the market, sends out a clear and understandable message. The book mirrors the changing times, wherein the world is taking a more ethical and accepting view of animals and focusing on *their* wellbeing, something that is often missing in traditional dog training.

In writing *Dog Knows*, Sindhoor has done a splendid job and has really hit the nail on the head! As the readers flip through the book, I hope they will not only enjoy but also learn from Sindhoor's wisdom.

Turid Rugaas
President of Pet Dog Trainers of Europe,
Dog Behaviourist, Author

PREFACE

My dog Nishi met with a horrific accident on a balmy day in February of 2011. A car ran over her face. Thankfully, she survived, but that incident changed our lives in ways we could never have imagined. Two years later, we got our second dog, Tiggy, who came with a history of severe early abuse. Nishi and Tiggy set us off on a long journey of understanding the meaning of pain, love and empathy. My search for answers led me to my mentors— Turid Rugaas, a canine ethology expert; Julia Robertson, a canine myotherapist; and the street dogs of India.

I got myself qualified as a behaviour consultant and a myotherapist. My studies on street dogs introduced me to the field of canine ethology. I then shed my avatar of an engineer, and my career with dogs began. As an ethological researcher, I aim to gain an understanding of the natural behaviour of free-willed dogs; as a behaviour consultant, I try to unravel the mind of the dog, working with behavioural clues that dogs offer; and as a myotherapist, I work on the body of the dog, observing the movements and gaits of dogs to develop a picture of their internal skeletal and muscular health and treating musculo skeletal issues through massages and functional movement. After having consulted with over 2,000 dogs, I set up an educational academy offering an accredited diploma on canine behaviour and ethology.

This book is a result of my learning journey. It is a narrative of my experiences with dogs, peppered with my professional insights into their lives, health and behaviour. Thanks to my engineering background, I have a scientific bent of mind, so when possible, I use studies to explain observed phenomena. Where science fails me, I simply present to you my observations and leave it up to you to draw conclusions. This is neither a cookbook on training dogs nor packed choc-a-bloc with scientific studies on dogs. The narrative is structured to focus on personal connection, with scientific corroboration wherever useful. References are provided wherever necessary, collated and listed on a website for easy access.

It is my understanding that animals are not simplistic beings that one can understand with simple theories. Dogs are complex beings, with rich social interactions and subtle communication. Their worldview is different from ours, and we may never fully comprehend it. I believe that we must humbly accept our limitations, whilst trying our best to understand them. We ought to marvel at what we do not understand and see if there are things that we can learn from them. Everything in nature has something to teach us. We are richer when we see ourselves as tiny cogs in a huge machine, and we must have the humility to learn from it.

CHAPTER 1

WE BECOME A FAMILY

Learning How to Learn from Dogs

My journey with animals started very early—with the dogs, cats and cows at my grandparents' farm in our village. Back then, my cousins and I were just excited about being in contact with animals, as most children are. Then my relationship with animals evolved to close friendships as my father started bringing home dogs and cats for us to care for as pets in our urban home.

Nishi walking into my adult life steered my journey in a new direction. The pressure to be a responsible pet parent obscured the organic nature of my connection with animals, and I set out on a mission to train my dog to be the best-behaved dog possible. However, a year into Nishi entering our lives, my journey took a tumultuous turn and drastically changed my outlook on my relationship with animals.

Dogs are remarkable creatures with incredible social skills with an impressive ability for conflict resolution and an uncanny ability to read humans and cooperate with us. The street dogs of India gave me an insight into their rich and complex social lives and their unique desire to coexist with humans. I went from wanting to teach my dog how to be a good dog to realizing that dogs are dogs. And it is not our place to judge animals and plants as *good* or *bad*. All animals want to be the best versions of themselves, and my job is to enable it for the ones in my care. But to bring out the best in my dogs, I had to learn to listen to them, understand the needs they express and meet those needs. I had to learn to shed my hubris on knowing what was best for dogs and to have the humility to embrace the idea that the dogs know what is best for them. I simply had to ensure they were in an environment where they could think and communicate clearly.

I had gone from wanting to train dogs to wanting to learn from dogs, but I found that it was not easy. I had to learn to shut up and observe, but silence is not exactly humankind's forte. I had to learn how to learn from dogs. This book chronicles my learning journey.

The First Encounter

Uttam and I leaned over the gate, trying to get a better look at the dark furballs—three boxer puppies. One was cowering under a table and looking up at us with big blue eyes. The other was in its own little world, fighting off imaginary monsters. The third was busy trying to figure out an escape route to come closer and examine us. I pointed at the escape artist and asked the man, 'What's her name?' 'Velvet,' he replied. Just one look at her coat glistening in the sun, and we knew why she had been named Velvet.

I looked at Uttam and tried to make as convincing a puppy dog face as the one that was hiding under the table. 'N.O. No! We are not taking home a puppy,' he said adamantly. 'You said we were here just to look at them, and that is all we are doing. So, look all you want,' he added.

The Rangapravesha

Around this time in 2010, I had just quit my corporate job, started working at an NGO and resumed my Bharatanatyam dance training. Indian classical dancers have one landmark solo performance called 'Rangapravesha', and mine was planned to be three hours long. Here I was, thirty years old, coaxing my adult muscles to move in ways they insisted were impossible. After months of practising for four to six hours a day, I was ready.

Eventually, the big day came. But my mind was elsewhere. I had managed to convince Uttam to bring home Velvet, and it was supposed to happen on the day after my Rangapravesha! But first, I had the daunting task of holding the attention of 200 people for three hours. And yet, every time I closed my eyes, I could only see the big blue eyes set in a ball of fur, eagerly scanning the compound to figure out how to escape and come to us.

When 4 p.m. came, I hit the stage shaking—half with excitement and half with anxiety. For the next three hours, my world was just that stage and nothing beyond. I gave that performance all I had to offer to the dancing part of my life, rather oblivious that I was living out the last few hours of my 'old life' and something new was taking shape. When the three hours were finally up, I walked in a daze and sat down exhausted, staring at my palms, my mind blank. I suddenly felt someone grab me and give me a big hug. It was Uttam. 'You were awesome!' he said. I snapped out of my trance. I had just completed my Rangapravesha!

The first sentence that slipped out of my mouth was, 'Velvet! Can we now go get her?' Uttam laughed and pointed to the audience. Friends and family were waiting. I dragged myself out and received their compliments with as much grace as I could muster. When I was finally done, out of my costume and into the car, it was 9 p.m. I asked Uttam again, 'Can we go pick up Velvet?' He laughed and said, 'Just rest today. We'll go tomorrow morning, first thing. I promise.' I drifted off to sleep as Uttam drove and had dreams of a puppy and myself on the stage.

Velvet Comes Home

The next morning, I woke up with a start and yelled, 'Velvet!' Uttam smiled and got out of bed, shaking his head. I could not wait. I was too excited to eat anything. So, we skipped breakfast, showered and left. These were the days before we were aware of adoptions, so we had unwittingly decided to buy a dog from a breeder.

When we reached the breeder's, I obviously pointed at Velvet and said, 'That one. I want that one.' I picked her up and—*crunch!*—she bit my nose. I was taken aback and looked down at her face. She was thrilled with what she had done and wagged her stub of a tail and licked me. I giggled and held her close.

Uttam held her while I got behind the wheel of the car and started driving. I could not get my eyes off her. I was so fixated on her that I almost ran the car into an autorickshaw. 'You sit with the puppy, I will drive,' said Uttam, a bit exasperated. I got in the passenger seat, placed a few sheets of newspaper on my lap, spread a towel and gingerly held Velvet on my lap. We were prepared for a carsick puppy and having to deal with a lot of mess. We were not prepared for what happened instead.

After the first few minutes, she started squirming until I let her go. She jumped off my lap and started exploring the inside of the car. She seemed to approve of everything, except the music. She barked a few puppy barks at the speakers. We changed the music a few times. She finally stopped barking when we played something she seemed to like. She then demanded to climb back up on to my lap to stare out the window. I rolled it down, and she was instantly half out of the car, enjoying her ears flapping in the wind. I then remembered having read that this was not good for dogs, as particles could go into their eyes and ears. I pulled her back in. She finally settled down and fell asleep. I looked at Uttam, a bit apprehensive of what he thought of this little fearless puppy. He was grinning from ear to ear.

A Mind of Her Own

At home, I had made meticulous preparations. The house was amply 'puppy-proofed'. I had read up a lot on what to expect and what to do. I had read that the most important thing is to draw boundaries on day one and be very disciplined about enforcing them. I was adamant that I was going to be a good pet parent and took all of this seriously. Having diligently done my homework, I was ready.

Or so I thought.

When Velvet walked into the house, she explored every inch of the house, taking stock of everything. She then walked straight up to us and demanded to be let on to the sofa. The resolve to draw strict boundaries melted away when we saw those big blue eyes. After exploring the sofa, she found a cosy spot under the coffee table and fell asleep, showing us rather unambiguously that she had a mind of her own and would be fearless about exercising her right to an opinion. Uttam smiled and said, 'Well! Thus, the puppy arrives.'

Uttam was thrilled with Velvet's entry into our lives. He was fascinated by this puppy who had loads of oomph and attitude. I had become a little less enthusiastic about this 'defiant puppy'. Imposing rules would be a lot harder on a dog that had a mind of her own. I started wondering if I would be stuck with an 'untrainable dog' who was going to cause more worry than bring joy. Was the honeymoon over? I wish someone had told me then that I would come to fall in love with this attitude and learn to work with it, not fear it.

For days prior to Velvet's arrival, we had been brainstorming what we would name her. 'Velvet' sounded like a stripper's stage name. We wanted to change that. We wanted something that was inspired by her dark colour. 'Nisha' in Sanskrit means the beautiful darkness of the night. But I wanted the name to end with an 'i' or 'y', because Indian names for girls tend to end in an 'i' or a 'y'. Basically, I wanted a name that sounded 'girly' because that makes a dog look less intimidating to people, and I wanted my puppy to have that advantage. We decided on Nishi.

I also wanted a name that could be drawn out when calling to her in a park: 'Neeeeeeeeeeesheeeeeeeeeeeee'. Little did we anticipate the various ways in which we would draw out this name—some seeped in pure joy, some out of complete frustration, some laden in pain and suffering. For now, Nishi-puppy was sleeping under the coffee table, blissfully dreaming puppy dreams, and for some reason, that just brought me a lot of joy.

The First Meal

Once she woke up, the first thing we did was take her to the garden to pee. Then, it was time to feed her. We had bought a bag of food that she was used to. We fed her some. She ate with enthusiasm, so much so that we felt she was still hungry. We fed her more. She gobbled that up too. We fed her even more. That too disappeared. She was now starting to look like a pregnant puppy. Uttam and I looked at each other. 'Should we stop?' 'Yeah. Perhaps. Let's go look up how much to feed her.' It had never occurred to us to have done that research before feeding her. Once we did, we found that commercial dry dog food expands significantly on soaking up water. We have also come to learn what goes into them and that it's not so wonderful for our dogs. It has been a long, enlightening journey.

All of this happened in 2010. Now that I have studied dogs extensively for years, I see how so many of my early decisions were terrible. But that is all part of being a pet parent. From being the idiot who overfed her puppy, I have come a long way. Today, I am a qualified canine behaviour consultant and canine myotherapist. I now have a career in canine care and am a lot more educated on topics that stumped me back then. In this book, in addition to sharing my follies as a naive pet parent, I share my perspective as a professional. So, when relevant, I will do a deep dive into some of these topics, presented to you as essays. This first is meant to help you work out a good diet for your dog.

CANINE NUTRITION

The nutritional requirement of an individual is driven by several factors, including the species, the individual's metabolism, other dynamic internal conditions like physical and mental health, as well as external conditions like weather and humidity. In a tropical country like India, it is easy to see that some days are simply too hot for certain foods, while some cold days make us crave specific foods. Our health, too, seems to impact our cravings and resistance to food. For example, stress is known to increase our craving for carbohydrates, while we may find some pain relief when we consume spicy foods. Then, there are food items that are considered to have anti-carcinogenic properties, anti-inflammatory properties, 'brain foods', etc.

My area of expertise is behaviour, and joint and muscle health. My concern with food is because food impacts the internal condition of the body, including gut health, stress hormone levels and inflammation in the body, all of which further impact health and behaviour. Food also impacts mood, which in turn impacts behaviour. There seem to be emerging interesting links between certain behaviours, such as excessive chewing and licking (oral stereotypes), and gut health and ulcers. Similarly, in my experience, digestive issues such as malabsorption can lead to severe anxiety around food and also result in biting. Food intolerances often seem to manifest as food faddism. Dental issues, ear infections and throat issues in dogs seem to make some foods impossible to consume. If not given an alternative, dogs may be seen fiddling with their food and nosing it around their bowl—unable to eat, yet unable to ignore their hunger.

All of these are dynamic, which makes the nutritious needs of an individual highly dynamic as well. My first recommendation is to move to a diet that allows the conscientious pet parent the flexibility to alter and change it based on the changing needs of the dog. My next recommendation is to either seek the advice of a qualified canine nutritionist or to educate yourself on the latest in the field of canine nutrition and functional foods, so as to be able to understand the dynamic nutritional needs of a dog and tailor the food to serve their current needs.

Canine nutrition experts aren't the only ones you can rely on. Interestingly, you can turn to dogs themselves for some guidance. Animals are known to be highly intuitive and in tune with the needs of their body. It has been observed that animals in the wild have not only an inherent instinct around what is the right food for them and what is toxic, but also the ability to build a 'pharmacy' by using different medicinal plants in their ecosystem to alleviate common health issues. It is not uncommon to observe street dogs exhibit similar discretion in their consumption of medicinal plants. The emerging field of Applied Zoompharmacognosy is the study of this knowledge in companion animals, and it is interesting to note that many of our domestic and companion animals seem to retain such abilities.

Of course, esoteric herbs and oils must always be used with adequate input from all relevant qualified professionals. But we can still learn to pay heed to the dogs' input on their daily dietary requirements, especially when working with fresh, natural, unprocessed, whole foods. For example, my dogs, especially when "recovering from" mild ailments, clearly demonstrate what they prefer—be it kefir, healing bone broth, regular bone broth, spices, complex carbohydrates, certain protein sources and specific textures. The only area I have seen their instincts fail repeatedly is when it comes to simple sugars and highly processed foods, or when they are in a frenzy. So, yes, don't feed your dogs sweets, refined breads, chocolates and such, irrespective of what those puppy-dog eyes seem to be telling you. Pet parents do need a basic understanding of what dogs can and cannot be fed. I have a collection of recommended readings on a dedicated website, which includes one on canine nutrition.

One last thing on self-selection of food: Do not expect a hyperactive dog or puppy to be paying close attention to what their body is telling them. Pet parents must also be investing time and effort into calming their dogs down, getting them to start thinking and taking good decisions for themselves. We will revisit this topic repeatedly in the book.

Ayurveda says that all health starts with gut health. While this may be an oversimplification, we cannot underestimate the role of good food in the physical and mental well-being of a dog.

Being a pet parent is not easy. After feeding Nishi poor-quality food in inappropriate quantities, which would make her tummy bloat, we, rather appropriately, started freaking out, worried to bits that her stomach would burst. Nishi, of course, seemed happily oblivious to our worry and was half-running, half-rolling on the floor—thrilled for no apparent reason. And thus, we made our first of many frantic calls to the vet.

Puppy Foraging

Over the next few months, we learnt that puppies explore the world with their curious little minds and pearly teeth. But when something disturbs their exploration sessions, they can get excited or agitated, and their developing instincts can fail them. They then end up doing strange things like running away with and gulping down the object of our attention. We once found a bulletin board pin in Nishi's poop. She must have been exploring it when we were exiting the lift. In our eagerness to leave, we must have rushed her, causing her to grab it and gulp it down! So there we were, making yet another frantic call to the vet.

Life was a non-stop adventure with Nishi. She came to us bang in the middle of mango season. Having watched *Marley and Me*, we were inspired to let her try out a mango. We too love mangoes and were eager to share with her something we loved so much. We picked the perfect day and the perfect mango for our perfect puppy. We excitedly trotted off to the garden and found the perfect spot to let our puppy explore this perfect fruit. You guessed it … it was going to be far from 'purrrrfect'.

Nishi was very excited about this new experience. For a long time, she fiddled around with the mango, not even breaking open the skin. It looked like she was just taking in the smell, shape and texture of this new object. Then, she bit in with her little sharp puppy teeth. The syrupy juice oozed out. She licked it up and her puppy eyes lit up. Quickly, she started peeling the fruit open and stuffing her face with the sweet mango pulp. Uttam and I smiled at each other, held hands and sighed like silly young couples do, gushing over the puppy and getting her overly excited about all of this.

At some point, we got lost in our 'silly new-couple conversation', saying sweet nothings to each other. Both Uttam and I lost track of what little Nishi was up to. Eventually, our sense of responsibility returned, and Uttam glanced at our mango-faced puppy. 'Erm … where is the seed?' he asked. Feeling like idiots— not for the first time since we got her—we frantically searched for the seed. No seed!

By now, the vet was on speed dial. We called him, late in the night, sheepishly explaining to him what had happened. He told us that we had to watch her closely for the next couple of days. The seed was too big for her to poop out. She would have to vomit it out. If not, we would have to get it surgically removed. He asked us to watch Nishi for loss of appetite, in case the seed got stuck in her digestive tract. We watched her like a hawk the next day. No vomit, no seed, no loss of appetite. We watched her the day after. And the day after. We watched her a whole week. No seed. Weeks passed. Still no seed. And yet, not a dent in her appetite. To this day, we have no idea what happened to the seed!

The mango seed was enough for me to freak out. So I went about puppy-proofing the house. I identified all objects that were of value to me or dangerous to my puppy, kissed them tenderly and told them that they all needed to go away for a few months. We set aside a room that we planned to leave her in when we went to work. The room had a balcony that she could pee in, in our absence. We cleared it of anything that she might possibly destroy. We moved all the furniture out of that room. However, puppy-proofing was only a part of the equation. If she had to manage without us at home, we would have to toilet-train her and teach her to stay alone. Nishi had entered a brand-new world entirely unfamiliar to her, and we had to gently induct our new puppy into our way of life.

A Whole New World

Uttam and I had saved up all our leave days. To welcome and induct Nishi into our family, we decided to use them all during this time. Between the two of us, we managed a month of someone being home and helping Nishi learn how to be part of our family.

Often, we don't realize what a big deal this is for a dog or a pup. Imagine having your world turned inside out overnight, no explanation given, and having to figure out every detail, starting with, 'Why am I here?' As humans, we can be made to understand that we are relocating, even if we don't really want to do it. Dogs need to figure out, at their own pace, that the new place is 'home' and that they are safe. We wanted to be there for Nishi while she figured this out.

Learning to Stay Home Alone

The first time we left Nishi alone was to attend a dinner at a friend's house upstairs. We waited until she was sound asleep in her bed and tip toed out of the room and out of the house. Just a few minutes after our arrival, Uttam and I were looking at each other with one question on our mind: Is Nishi okay? Gah! We could not take it any more and decided to go check on her.

Uttam was about to unlock the door when I stopped him. 'Don't! It'll wake her up. Shh. Listen.' There was not a sound in the house. We took that as a sign of her being asleep and went back up. This was ten minutes after we had first arrived. Over the next hour, one of us kept going down every ten minutes to check on her. Finally, our hosts saw our plight and let us off the hook. We ran down, opened the main door and burst into the room Nishi was in, only to find her passed out, all four legs in the air, blissfully unaware of the trauma we had put ourselves through.

After that, we gained the confidence to start making small trips outside the house during the day. Nothing more than five minutes at a time— downstairs to take a call, or to the local store to pick up chillies. Eventually, five minutes became ten, ten minutes became twenty, twenty minutes became an hour. After that, it was smooth sailing. We increased Nishi's 'alone time' by twenty additional minutes each day, until our month was up and we had to go back to work. I went to work early and returned early. Uttam went to work late and returned late. So we made sure that Nishi was not home alone for more than six hours at a time. She managed just fine. I suspect she just slept.

Working Parents' Guilt

In the beginning, I felt terrible about the idea of Nishi sleeping all day in the apartment. Like many others, I believed that dogs needed a lot of space, lacking which, they at least needed something to keep them engaged. My father and grandfather kept dogs outside their houses. So, in my mind, being 'indoor dogs' in an apartment translated to dull dogs that were bored out of their wits all day. Then, I learnt two things about my guilt. First, my guilt was translating into behaviours and body language that made Nishi anxious and excitable, which was becoming a roadblock in teaching her to stay at home alone. Second, I learnt that the guilt was entirely unnecessary, because many dogs can benefit from some 'alone time' to catch up on sleep!

UNDERSTANDING SLEEP

Sleep is not an indulgence. Sleep is sometimes likened to an upgrade from economy to business class. It's not. It's not even an upgrade from economy to first class. The critical thing to realize is that if you don't sleep, you don't fly. Essentially, you never get there, and that's what's extraordinary about much of our society these days is that we are desperately sleep-deprived.'
—Dr Russell Foster, Neuroscientist and Head, Sleep and Circadian Neuroscience Institute

We all know that sleep is essential for wellness, but it is more than just that. Sleep is essential for *survival*. The brain is a fuel-guzzling organ that consumes 20–25 per cent of the total calories utilized by a person, even though it counts for only 3 per cent of our total body weight. All the organs in the body that consume calories for metabolism generate by-products that need continuous clearing, which is done by the lymphatic system. However, the brain has its own housekeeping system that requires the organ to shut down. Cerebrospinal fluid resides around the brain and enters the brain for clearing the metabolites and toxins that build up. This scheduled 'maintenance shutdown' is sleep.

Think of a massive power plant that is shut down for housekeeping. As you can well imagine, that is not a simple process. The same is true of sleep. More than half of sleep goes into powering down the brain and shutting it down slowly. This part of sleep is called 'shallow sleep'. Interestingly, of the remaining, only about half is used for housekeeping, which is called 'slow wave sleep', indicative of the slower nature of the brain waves during this period. The other half is called 'REM (Rapid Eye Movement) sleep', which is dedicated to memory consolidation and learning. The brain does most of this by replaying the actions of the day, making sense of it and selectively storing what it deems are the most important lessons learnt. During this phase of sleep, the brain suddenly becomes very active.

New neural pathways are created—building a library of knowledge ranging from mundane activities, such as walking or driving, to more complicated tasks, such as social interaction with others and problem-solving. These are refined over time. This complicated process is what we come to recognize as dreaming.

That's right, dogs dream too. So do rats.

Of course, most pet parents have always suspected that animals dream. We have noticed the classic tell tale signs of dreaming, which look like they are running, whimpering or eating in their sleep. Often, when in REM sleep, they may stretch out to enable these movements.

So, how much sleep do dogs need? This is quite subjective, not only varying from individual to individual but also influenced by several extrinsic factors such as age and health. However, there is a common consensus that the human requirement for sleep averages somewhere around eight hours. With dogs, this requirement seems to be almost double. This could be attributed to the fact that they spend less than 10 per cent of their total sleep in REM sleep, which is less than half of that in humans. What happens if we don't get enough sleep or good quality sleep? Of course, we are all aware that if we feel like we have not slept enough, we tend to get cranky or are not very productive. However, the long-term consequences seem far more dire.

Dogs assume different positions. Some may curl up during deep sleep or stretch out during REM sleep. But sleeping positions may also depend on the ambient temperature or internal physical or emotional health of the dog.

Dogs exposing their belly makes them extremely vulnerable. They only dare to sleep like this if they are feeling completely relaxed and secure. But if they do this when they are awake, it may be communicating extreme fear and a sign of begging to not be hurt. Read other body language cues to see if they are relaxed or tense.

Below are some of the consequences of sleep deprivation on organisms:

1. **Cognition**: When we don't get enough sleep, particularly REM sleep, there is insufficient memory consolidation. 'Learning' is a process of progressively building on top of ideas, which is not possible if the previous ideas were not consolidated and stored properly. Thus, overall learning is altered.

2. **Immunity**: A big part of the immune function of the body is carried out by white blood cells, the release of which is dependent on the internal sleep clock of an animal. Consequently, poor sleep unravels an organism's immunity. The extent of this can be understood by considering that the WHO has officially declared 'night-shift' as a carcinogen!

3. **Stress**: Stress and sleep have an unholy relationship and can create a vicious cycle. Any surge in stress and excitement increases adrenaline and cortisol in the body. Cortisol impedes sleep. A decrease in sleep time reduces the amount of cortisol cleared in the body, which in turn makes the individual more susceptible to feeling stressed in everyday situations.

4. **Growth**: When the brain is in its housekeeping phase, growth hormones are released which help in the repair and replacement of body tissues. Additionally, brain cells are constantly being

replaced by a process known as 'neurogenesis'.
Sleep deprivation negatively impacts both.

5. **Death**: Sleep deprivation can cause death by auto-intoxication of the brain. In the case of dogs, this can take anywhere from nine to fourteen days.

WHAT IMPEDES SLEEP IN DOGS

1. **Disruption:** Dogs need almost sixteen hours of sleep, and a large part of it happens during the day. As pet parents, we often keep waking our dogs up. Sleep occurs in stages and an organism moves from stage to stage, falling deeper and deeper into sleep and gradually coming out of it, over a cycle of 90–110 minutes (in humans), which keeps repeating itself. The exact duration of this cycle in dogs is currently unknown, but the pattern is believed to be similarly cyclical. So, if a dog is being woken up constantly, they are not completing a full sleep cycle and may remain in shallow sleep. We've already seen the importance of these deeper stages of sleep.

2. **Hormones:** Adrenaline and cortisol impede sleep. These are typically generated because of excessive excitement, anxiety or fear, all of which seem to dominate urban life.

3. **Discomfort:** How many times have we woken up saying we have had a bad night of sleep because we were either lying on a bed that was too hard, the weather was too cold or too hot, or we were

not able to stretch enough? Feeling safe and secure also seems to be an important determinant when it comes to feeling comfortable.

4. **Light:** The body maintains an internal clock called a 'circadian rhythm' which dictates when an animal should be sleeping and when they should be awake. This clock is closely related to the exposure to various components present in natural light. Change in light—either insufficient exposure to natural light or untimely exposure to artificial light—can alter the circadian rhythm and thus affect the quality of sleep.

HOW TO IMPROVE SLEEP IN DOGS

1. **Provide comfortable beds:** Comfort is highly subjective and is based on personal preference. Some dogs prefer elevated surfaces, while some prefer the cool floor and yet others prefer cosy corners. Some days, a dog might find their usual bed too hot to sleep on, while on others they may feel the bed isn't warm enough. Sometimes, they may want to curl up, and at other times, they may need to stretch out. Since there is not one right answer to the kind of bed dogs prefer, the best way to enable good sleep is to provide a host of different options and provide the dog the freedom to be able to choose.

2. **Reduce cortisol:** Cortisol can be a direct result of either excitement or fear in dogs. So, both

hyperactive and anxious dogs will struggle to get sufficient sleep, which in turn can exacerbate their excitement or anxiety. Avoiding an adrenaline-inducing lifestyle is the first step. In addition, activities such as sniffing, chewing and eating as well as a few foods are known to reduce cortisol. These are discussed in a later essay.

3. **Don't wake them up:** While this might seem obvious, it's harder than you would imagine. Humans get their eight or nine or ten hours of sleep at one stretch, when we turn off the lights, shut off all distractions and put ourselves in the most comfortable, secure situation to get our sleep. However, dogs sleep almost twice as much, and this is spread across the day. Thus, they are sleeping in an environment filled with sounds of the doorbell ringing, phone ringing, footsteps of people walking up and down the house, the inescapable screech of the pressure cooker going off ... the list goes on. This is why we should not feel guilty about leaving our dogs home alone for a few hours during the day.

4. **Give them a sense of security:** While leaving a dog home alone can give them some peace and allow them to sleep, leaving them outdoors or confined is not advisable. Left outdoors, their alerting instincts kick in and they simply cannot sleep in peace. It can also get too noisy and distracting. However, even indoor dogs need

access to a range of spaces where they seem most comfortable. Interestingly, while our presence during the day could hamper their sleep, during the night, it could improve it. Dogs are social sleepers, sharing the responsibility of keeping watch. Sleeping alone may mean shouldering all that responsibility by themselves. Our presence in the night can often help them relinquish that responsibility, which can improve sleep.

5. **Provide sleep-inducing food:** Some foods (complex carbohydrates, certain fats, foods containing tryptophan and melatonin) are known to induce sleep and may be good temporary solutions to highly stressed-out or hyperactive dogs. A few herbs and essential oils are known to help, but these must be used with caution. A dog's sense of smell is very powerful and such scents can have undesired consequences. Your dog must always have the option of walking away from these herbs and oils. For particularly restless dogs, a vet may be able to prescribe drugs as the last resort.

It is a healthy habit to periodically do a sleep study on your dogs to objectively track the number of hours they sleep and how many times they are woken up in a day. The first step to improving anything is to understand it.

Crate Training

We got Nishi a crate. I had read about it being very important in training. Growing up, we had never heard of crates. I was not really sure what to do with it or what kind of crate I needed. I went to the store and got her the biggest, fanciest one I could find. I had read up about how it kept them safe and helped with toilet training, simulating the comfort of a den. It sounded so amazing that I wondered how I had even managed to have dogs without this magic contraption.

Having completed the initial training, I decided to use it to confine her for a bit when the housekeeper was mopping the house. I put her in there. She cried. She barked. She protested. I tried everything I had learnt about crate training … nothing worked. She kept at it until the lady was done mopping and I let Nishi out. She walked out, gave me a long stare, took two tiny steps with her tiny paws, walked away and sat facing away from me. I felt miserable. I sat next to her and tried to play with her. She got up, sighed, walked away from me and sat facing away again. This happened a few times, and I suddenly realized, 'Oh my goodness! This puppy is actually angry with me.' She had suddenly gone from being a cute, furry playmate to having actual emotions, opinions and the right to disagree with me.

Nishi's message was very clear: 'I do not like being put in that box.' When I was growing up, I saw my grandfather and father express a general distaste towards confining animals, explaining to me that animals did not like that. So, it did not seem to be a particularly unreasonable request from Nishi, and I gave in. I'll admit that I did not really put effort into crate training her properly, but I am glad I did not. I no more see any need for it, and advocate against it.

A CLOSER LOOK AT CRATES

An article published by PETA tries to trace back the history of using crates and says, 'Crating began as a way for people who participate in dog shows to keep their dogs clean, but they did not take into account their dogs' social, physical, and psychological needs.' Subsequently, the use of crates may have become more prevalent during the world war, for transporting war dogs and further more in the context of air travel in more recent times. But it is only rather recently that there seems to have been a push to introduce crate usage at homes in some countries, perhaps as a way to expand to new market segments. Today, crates have almost become mandatory for dog owners in the US. However, they are not as popular in many other countries, and in some countries, there are restrictions around confinement areas. In Finland and Sweden, crates are illegal. People who continue to use crates today do it for two main reasons: to keep the puppy out of trouble and because it is believed that dogs are den animals who feel safer in crates.

During my street dog studies, discussed in Chapter 6, I noticed that some streeties tend to dig out den-like structures in sand piles or opt to sleep under cars or inside drains. Some scared dogs retreat under a bed or a table. But they don't seem to want to use these nooks all the time. More often, streeties prefer to sleep on elevated surfaces or in open spaces where they can have plenty of company. Typical 'den animals' live most of their lives in dens, but free-ranging dogs use these spaces sparingly and only when they have a choice to walk in and out at will.

As a part of my education, we did sleep studies on our own pet dogs and found that dogs are polyphasic sleepers; given the freedom to do so, dogs get up between their bursts of sleep and move about. In the previous essay on sleep, I explain that comfort is important to improve the quality of sleep and the dangers of not getting sufficient good-quality sleep. Dogs use the surface they sleep on for temperature regulation too, which they cannot do unless they can move out of the confines of a crate. There are studies that show that confinement increases stress and lead to behavioural issues.

It's true that keeping a dog in crates can keep them out of trouble and possible self-harm. However, given the damage it can do to their sleep, health, behaviour and musculature, I find puppy-proofing, puppy pens and lifestyle changes to be safer options. This is not really very difficult for us in India, because we have traditionally never used this piece of equipment.

The only scenario where it may be impossible to avoid using crates is during air travel. In such cases, it is important to slowly and systematically get your dog used to tolerating the crate without getting overly stressed. Since dogs are not really den animals, most of them are not naturally comfortable in crates and need a gentle introduction. Crates can get so stressful for some dogs in this situation that they might not make it through the long journey. So exercise extreme caution and take time to gently and gradually get your dog used to this piece of equipment.

Suiting Up

Through all our learnings, Nishi was growing up rapidly. As she started getting faster on her furry little paws, we could no longer take her to the garden without a leash on. She would take off the minute we reached the garden and run into the hedges. As much as we would have liked following her, scurrying off under the hedges was not possible. Not that it kept us from trying.

When the little escape artist we had on our hands was contemplating the world outside our compound with curiosity, we realized that the puppy that had tried to escape the breeder's premises a few months ago to come meet us was now growing and wanted to meet the world. We could not prevent her from doing that. But it had to be done with her safety in mind. So, we went hunting for walking equipment. It was time to suit up!

The first advice we were given was that we had to get Nishi on a choke collar. We were told that she would soon get big and strong, and that I would not be able to handle such a big dog. We were recommended to give the 'tough' lessons early on, so that it could be 'tough enough'. Except, we just didn't know how to be tough on a puppy. On our first walk with a 'choke' collar, we saw it do exactly that—*choke* Nishi. The first breath that she struggled to take made us gasp too. She was too small and frail a pup to be experiencing something like that. That was that. We took the collar off, picked her up and walked back home. The collar became only ornamental, to hang a name tag on it when we went swimming—making her look like an '80s Kannada movie villain.

The next thing we were told was to put Nishi on a flat collar. We did. We headed out on our merry walk. By now, Nishi had started to get a hang of 'walks' and was excited by the idea. This made her dart out. The collar stopped her by yanking back on her neck. I am sure that hurt her. I have tried putting a collar on my neck and pulling at half that strength—it hurt! I have since learnt about the anatomy of the dog enough to know that there's no reason it should not hurt a dog as well. No wonder she stopped dead on her tracks and turned and looked at us with a look of surprise, as if she did not know where the pain came from and why it hurt. To this day, that look of hers haunts me. By now you know our drill. We took off the collar, picked her up and brought her back home.

My sister's husband (then boyfriend) told us to consider this thing called a 'body belt' or a harness. 'It does not go around the neck. It goes around the chest, which is really a much stronger part of the dog's body,' he told us. With my current understanding of canine anatomy, I can verify that his reasoning was sound and am ever grateful for his inputs. After we got her a harness, we have not looked back. We did toy around a lot with the types of harnesses and have settled on what we like. At the end of this chapter, I have added an essay on harnesses, approaching it from a scientific perspective rather than just us gasping at our puppy gasping. At this point, I'll just move on with the story because the next part is interesting.

The Date

One evening, after we had taught Nishi how to stay home alone, Uttam suggested we take a break and go out on a dinner date. 'Just a nice date, like we used to when we first started dating,' he said. I reluctantly agreed. I hated being away from Nishi. 'Wear something nice,' Uttam said. 'Oh! Where are we going? Can't we just go to the local bar? I'll come in my jeans and tee,' I snapped. He smiled and said, 'It's a surprise. It will be my treat.' I decided to relax, take it easy and go with the flow. I wore a nice red dress and got into the car with him, which smelt of dog and was lined with 'dog glitter', more commonly known as 'dog fur'.

Uttam took me to one of the fanciest restaurants in the city. I looked at him and smiled. A puppy had not been all fun and games. It had been hard work. It had been about poop and pee and drool. It had been about early-morning and late-evening walks, without the luxury of missing a single day—not for drinks with friends, not for a hangover. It had become about dead social lives. This was a welcome break.

A little after we were seated, Uttam went down on one knee! 'Oh no. Oh no. Is this what I think it is? No no no!' I said and burst into tears. 'No?' Uttam looked surprised. He cocked his head to one side like Nishi docs when she hears strange sounds. 'Is this what I think it is?' I asked again. 'Sindhoor, will you marry me?' he asked, looking a bit nervous and confused. 'Of course I will!'

After I had managed to get over my crying, announcing to half the restaurant that I had just been proposed to, calling my sister and finally settling down for that dinner we had come to have, I asked Uttam, 'I have a nagging suspicion that Nishi has something to do with this proposal. Am I right?' 'Yeah. She does. I've known you since college and I thought I had seen every facet of you, and I loved it all. But she has brought out yet another side of you that I love. I want to be with you for the rest of my life.' I cried again. For the hundredth time or so that night. And I was not done. I came home, sat next to Nishi and cried again. She had given me the best gift of my life—my marriage.

WALKING EQUIPMENT

Fastening restraining equipment around animals' necks is a very ancient idea. However, the impact of this practice on the animal had not been sufficiently studied until recently. Today, there is enough evidence to suggest that the use of restraints around the neck has severe short- and long-term implications. I have listed several of these studies in the reference section on our website, but we should not really need studies to tell us what common sense can.

If you think about it, the neck is the most vulnerable part of a vertebrate's body. It has some very important functions, and yet, unlike the heart or the brain, it is not encased in a bony cover. Animals exploit this exact vulnerability when hunting and going for the kill: it's almost always the neck. Without having to read the

rest of this essay, you surely know that the only way
to strangle someone to death is to go for the neck.
What makes the neck so vulnerable? Let's examine the
anatomy of a mammal's neck to understand this better.
I invite you to start this discovery by placing your finger
on your neck and feeling around it a little bit.

Start with what is right under your fingers, beneath
the skin. The easiest to feel is perhaps the windpipe or
the trachea, which feels like a flexible ribbed pipe. It is a
critical structure that carries oxygen from the nose and
the mouth into the lungs. The trachea, made of cartilage,
is quite soft and can collapse easily when pressed.
Even the slightest pressure on it feels uncomfortable.
A compressed trachea is easily audible as laboured
breathing, which is noticeable when dogs are wearing
collars and are pulled on the leash. This tells us that the
trachea is exposed to mechanical damage not only in
humans but also in dogs.

The neck is the highway that carries blood—and thus
oxygen—to the eyes, ears and the brain. These important
arteries and veins are exposed on the neck such that any
pressure can cut off circulation, as evidenced by the
tongues of dogs turning blue when they pull too hard
on a collar and leash. Unfortunately, unlike most other
parts of the body, the brain and eyes are very sensitive to
oxygen being cut off, even for very short periods of time.
A study by A.M. Pauly, E. Bentley, K.A. Diehl and P.E.
Miller concluded that 'pressure in the eyes' increased

significantly from the baseline values when a force was applied to the neck via a leash to a collar. This does not happen with harnesses. Julia Robertson, a canine anatomy expert and the pioneer of Galen Myotherapy for dogs, says, 'Reducing good flow of blood to and from the brain will have an impact on hormonal delivery, which can be catastrophic for the function of the senses: eyes, ears and nose.'

The neck is also home to several very soft organs. The lymph glands and the thymus have to do with the immunity of the body. Mechanical damage to these organs can compromise the overall immunity of the body, exposing dogs to several diseases. The thymus is particularly enlarged in puppies, making the gland even more vulnerable to damage. The thyroid gland is a butterfly-shaped soft organ located at the base of the neck, without much protection. Physical damage to this organ can impact its functioning, typically resulting in hypothyroidism in dogs. The condition is irreversible and has far-reaching consequences on the dog's health and behaviour for the rest of its life. More bad news here is that subclinical hypothyroidism is not easy to detect in its early stages. In her book *The Canine Hypothyroid Epidemic*, Dr Jean Dodds argues that the incidences of hypothyroidism are so high in our companion animals, the condition can be fairly called an 'epidemic'.

Then there is the hyoid bone, also known as the tongue bone. It is a dainty bone, and looking at it, it is not difficult to imagine how easily it can crack or break. Unfortunately, this goes unnoticed most times because pet owners rarely suspect a broken hyoid bone. When this bone is broken, it manifests as strange behaviours, such as abnormal appetite, abnormal water consumption and general irritation, which very few people associate with collar damage. Apart from discomfort when drinking water and eating food, the tongue is also important for movement. 'There is a muscle just above the dog's chest that stabilizes the tongue; if this muscle is disturbed or damaged it will affect the position of the tongue and this will impact the dog's total's balance,' says Julia Robertson.

If you continue inwards, you will reach the very core of the neck. This is the vertebral column. It is a misleading term, because one might picture a column. However, this is not a solid bone but a delicate chain of interlocking bone pieces—highly vulnerable to shear forces that can damage the interlocking, causing osteoarthritis of the spine or herniation of the disks. Julia explains, 'If a dog wearing a collar is being pulled sideways, this can cause something similar to whiplash injury which is due to the weight of the head and a sideways thrust. This type of force is not something the head can cope with from a functional perspective, and can very easily be damaged. This can leave dogs with permanent or in some cases a repetitive whiplash pain.' The vertebral column houses the spinal cord. The spinal cord is the information highway of the body, connecting the brain to the rest of the body. Nerves exit this highway on either side of the vertebrae, starting right at the base of the skull. Mechanical damage to this part can impinge on the nerves, causing pain. It can also impair other neurological functions.

Surrounding the vertebra in the neck are several muscles connecting the head to the chest, shoulders and legs. Despite being strong, these muscles are not immune to mechanical damage, as found in a study conducted in 1992 by Anders Hallgren. 'The clearest correlation in the study was between neck damages and jerk pull. 91 per cent of the dogs who had neck injuries had also experienced jerking of the leash.' Mechanical pressure on the belly of these muscles can not only damage the fine muscle fibres in it, but also have a cascading effect on all other parts of the neck and the parts that these muscles are connected to, including the head and the legs. This can lead to referred pain, and later, in a tingling sensation in the paws, which might also lead to dogs licking their paws.

Julia explains this cascading effect thus:

Damaged muscle fibres shorten during their self-healing mechanism. The shortening of the muscle length surrounding the vertebrae will draw these vertebrae of the neck closer together; in turn compromising the gap between each of the vertebral bodies, thereby impinging on the structures. This can have a devastating effect on the major nerves and the vessels supported through and around these vital vertebrae, with a high potential of severe dysfunction, pain and referred pain. Manifestations include deep physical and psychological effects; anyone who suffers from headaches from a bad neck will know how this feels.'

At this point, indulge me by placing two fingers on your neck and start pressing into your neck. It is likely to get quite uncomfortable quite quickly. Pain and discomfort are nature's way of preventing us from doing

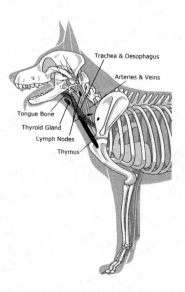

The neck is a very sensitive area with several critical organs that remain exposed to external damage. This is why we do not wear a seatbelt around our neck.

potentially harmful things to the body, like perhaps strapping a car seat belt around our own neck.

Now that you understand the anatomy of the neck, you will appreciate its fragility. The neck is just as valuable to a dog (and to all animals) as it is to us. Therefore, I do not recommend any equipment that needs to be fastened around an animal's neck. While I recommend harnesses as a safer alternative, it is important to point out that not all harnesses are safe. The following are some of the important considerations to make while trying to pick an ergonomically superior harness for your dog.

1. Dogs requires a full range of movement of the various joints and limbs. In Chapter 8, I have included an essay on the front leg that explains how the front legs of a dog are actually floating limbs, with the shoulder blade gliding over the ribcage. A harness that has straps that pass over the shoulders of a dog can restrict this gliding movement and result in improper loading of the joints, which can lead to long-term muscle and joint pain. A good harness, therefore, will steer clear of the shoulder blade.

2. Some harnesses tend to pinch under the armpits, which can cause chafing and irritation. It is better for a harness to move its straps further back down the rib cage, leaving the front limbs completely free.

3. Some harnesses have a metal clasp for attaching the leash on the front of the dog's body rather than the back. This can cause inadvertent damage to the spine, especially when the dog bolts. Even the most well-trained dog may bolt if there is a sudden loud noise or perhaps a cat or a squirrel in sight.

4. A good harness should not ride up high on the neck, since that can pinch on the neck like collars do. The whole point of using a harness is to shift the load down towards the sternum, which cannot be achieved by a harness that rides high on the neck.

5. For countries such as India, there is an additional consideration that harnesses must be as light and minimally covering as possible, so as to not overheat dogs. If you put your hand under the harness after a walk, it should not have heated up.

6. Some harnesses restrict the movement of the head and impose a certain head carriage. Unnatural head carriage causes muscular issues, as discussed in the essay on 'The Floating Limb' in Chapter 8. This type of harness can also cause neck injuries in dogs. 'I have seen some of the most awful whiplash injuries from these,' says Julia. 'The leverage potential on the dog's head through the joint where the skull meets the neck vertebra is huge! And the dog is anatomically really unprotected in this region.'

CHAPTER 2

EARLY EDUCATION

A Fresh Perspective on 'Problem Behaviours'

In 2013, I was lucky enough to start my education with Turid Rugaas, a world-renowned canine ethology expert, who was the first to document the calming signals of dogs. During our education with her she encouraged us to learn about dogs by observing them. This inspired me to launch a project called 'Lives of Streeties'. The first phase of this project spanned three years and 700 observations of street dogs, with the intent of learning about their activity budget. Some very interesting observations emerged from this project, one of them being a distinct difference in the behaviour of street dogs and pet dogs. These, however, were not the kinds of differences that people are commonly led to believe.

As a new pet parent, one piece of advice I received consistently and repeatedly was that I had to start training Nishi early. Failing to do so, I was told, would lead to umpteen behavioural issues. In fact, my profession is built on the backs of these very problems. As a practitioner, the most common of these problems that I have seen are dogs jumping on people, nipping people, barking excessively, destroying things, stealing things, inappropriately toileting, and reactivity or biting humans or other dogs. My observation of street dogs showed me that streeties rarely exhibit these 'problem behaviours'.

Toileting in inappropriate areas is not really relevant to street dogs. However, people who adopt 'ex-streeties' will often find that these dogs are already 'toilet-trained'. When Tiggy came to us, I wanted her to have a place in the house to use in case she needed to go when I was not at home. Since we get very good sunlight in India, the balconies are great for this. The house does not stink, and it's easy to wash the balcony each morning with a bucket of water. But nope! Tiggy would insist that she would only pee outside. While there are exceptions to this rule, most streeties that are allowed into homes do not pee or poop indoors.

Now imagine this. The doorbell rings, a Labrador bounds up to the door before anyone can reach it and the second the door is opened, the Labrador is jumping up on the guest, much to the embarrassed apologies of the owners. How familiar is this overenthusiastic Labrador greeting? I ask most people who interact with street dogs if they get similar greetings, and almost always, that is not the case. It is very rare to find a street dog who jumps up on people or nips them when playing with them. A few do, but they are really rare and not anywhere as much as our pet dogs. Who trains these streeties?

I remember a client who wanted my help to teach his streety not to rip up bike seat covers. Someone had done something nasty to this streety, and since then, the dog had taken to destroying bike seat covers. The reason this story stands out for me is that in all my professional experience, that was the only case of this kind involving a streety. Streeties do not really rip things up that often. If they did, with an army of more than 3,00,000 streeties in Bangalore alone, no bike would be spared. Streeties rarely destroy things, but our pet dogs are notorious for it.

Consider dogs eating junk. It's not at all uncommon for clients to complain that their dog eats paper or plastic or other inedible stuff. Isn't that strange considering there is perhaps not a species on earth (not yet, at least) that eats plastic? Our streeties do not find plastic edible. You cannot go feed a streety a bowl full of plastic and expect him to eat it. Sure, cows in India with no access to fodder eat plastic, but that's because there is often food in it, which they cannot separate out. Streeties are skilled at extracting food out of the plastic containers they are thrown in and are often seen doing so meticulously. No organism needs to be told what is food and what is not. However, pet dogs seem to be the only exception to this rule.

I believe my point is clear. Streeties do not seem to have so many of these 'problem behaviours' that our pet dogs do. But, when streeties get adopted and become pet dogs, several of these behaviours seem to surface in them quite quickly. Why? Is it really a lack of training or is it something else? It turns out that each of these behaviours is a complex response to internal needs of a dog and warrants closer examination—something I did not realize until I did my study on street dogs.

Time Lost

When I first got Nishi, I had not done my 'Lives of Streeties' project. So I had not asked myself about the origin of these so-called 'bad behaviours'. Instead, I was preoccupied with preventing or extinguishing these behaviours. In my desire to create the 'perfect dog', I simply dived headlong into the dizzying world of training. I learnt about very technical terms such as positive/negative, punishment/reward, clickers, clicker charging, treat-value grading. I diligently learnt it all and made elaborate training plans. I calibrated my treats into high-value and low-value ones. I had plans for gradually building difficulty levels. I felt like I was drowning in rules, excel sheets and treats.

As I write this chapter, I am sitting in the lap of nature, in a place called Swarga, in the Malnad region of south India. It has been our favourite family vacation spot for almost a decade, mostly because of how much our dogs love it. Nishi is now old, almost blind, unable to move—making us painfully aware that this might be one of our last times there as a family. We have been reminiscing about all the times we have been here over the last decade. Despite the countless wonderful memories, a sense of guilt overwhelms me. I think of all the time I lost trying to impose the rules of my training on Nishi. I distinctly recall the times I insisted that she needed to practise leash discipline, instead of letting her be a dog and enjoy such a wonderful part of the world.

Turid often says, 'Life is not obedience training.' I feel sad about the time I lost not understanding that. Today, as we grasp at each moment we have left with Nishi, each memory we can continue to make, I regret not having lived life to the fullest in my quest to impose rules. There was another way.

A decade of life with Nishi, and I have now learnt that the skills she really needed were not how well she obeyed us. Despite all my spreadsheets and treats and techniques, Nishi never really was good at following commands. But she has other skills, ones that I have come to see as far more valuable. She has incredible conflict-resolution skills with other dogs. She is an extremely confident dog, who bounces back from all kinds of fear remarkably quickly. She is amazing with puppies and helped us with several of our foster puppies, patiently and gently drawing them out of their shell. She is a fantastic mentor to younger dogs. She is an extremely sensitive dog who is excellent at sensing my moods and knowing exactly when to cheer me up or sit reassuringly by my side. She is an extremely gentle soul, mindful of what bothers others. She trusts us completely to provide her the care she needs, even if it causes her some temporary discomfort. Despite going to hell and back, she retains her positive attitude, her faith in humans and her unbridled joie de vivre.

None of my efforts could have trained any of this into her—things that, in the end, are all that matters. I could have spent my time recognizing these in her and celebrating them. Instead, I spent it being stressed out about not being able to train her to do things that she eventually never learnt to do, which, I can say confidently, never really mattered.

Problem Solving and Boundary Setting

When I talk about not training my dogs, people assume I mean that there are no boundaries in my home and that it is pure chaos. Some assume that my dogs do not have any of the 'problem behaviours' that we see so often in pet dogs. Neither is true. Like all companion dogs, mine too exhibited these problems.

Nishi was an intense jumper. When it started, it was inconspicuous. But as she grew up to become a very big, heavy, persistent, strong dog, who loves people, it got really bad. Basically, I had a massive dog hurtling herself at people, resulting in bruises and scratches! That's not fun for anyone, so my social circle started dwindling. Big dog owners will relate to this. I started asking people to meet me at the local bar instead of inviting them home, because Nishi's jumping was out of hand. I needed a solution.

Puppy Nishi was also a nipper. Remember the little bite Velvet had landed on my nose? At the time, I had giggled. As Velvet became Nishi, and Nishi grew, those bites were no longer amusing. From giggling, I was now yelping in pain.

I had just got my nose pierced. And Nishi found my nose stud particularly attractive to chew on, to the point where, one day, she nicked it so bad that my nose started to bleed. I was nervous that she had successfully done what I had paid the jeweller to do: puncture my nose. 'Would I now have to wear two nose studs? How would that look?' I wondered as I tried to take stock of the damage. Lucky for me, it was not that bad.

Later in the book, we will delve into a story that explains why Nishi went on to develop a severe fear of other dogs, resulting in her frequently lunging at them. Nishi also used to pull quite a bit on the leash, and I have fallen flat on my face many a time, trying to walk a dog almost two-thirds my body weight. Our second dog, Tiggy, came with the issue of growling at people and destroying everything in sight. We did have our share of 'problem behaviours', and I am glad to admit that we do not have to live with these problems anymore. The solution, however, was not as simple as training it all out of the dog. With each of them, it has taken me deep introspection on what was leading to these behaviours. Understanding the origin of these behaviours led me to solutions. Through the course of this book, I will systematically present this understanding and several of my ideas.

Inconvenient Connection Seeking

Dogs will often seek connection by jumping, nipping or barking. Most people do not appreciate these behaviours, and, it turns out, neither do dogs. Remember my study on street dogs? While puppies often exhibit these behaviours, adult streeties rarely do. So, I decided to observe streeties and try to understand what was going on here.

Animals need care, more so the young ones. It could be care in terms of nourishment, warmth, social interaction or attachment. These are all considered inelastic connection-needs of an individual, meaning those that are important for survival. While several of these needs may change as animals grow, they will still have connection-needs that must be met by other individuals, particularly for social beings. Animals have ways to express these needs, and these care-seeking behaviours are what we call 'et-epimeletic behaviours'. Puppies are born in a litter. To compete for their mother's attention, they may engage in et-epimeletic behaviours like jumping, nipping or whining. Adult dogs will often meet the needs of the puppies when puppies engage in this behaviour. But after the puppies reach a certain age, adult doggies are very good at telling their pups that while they still intend to meet their connection-needs, they have outgrown the behaviours they are using to express the need and must find other ways to do so.

Unfortunately, when dogs come to live with us, neither do we recognize these behaviours for what they represent, nor do we know how to convey to their dog that they need to find more appropriate ways of expressing needs. For example, dogs may jump on us or bark at us to express that they are seeking social connection with us or simply need to be let out to pee. What I have observed in my clients is that most get rather annoyed with the way the dog is expressing that need, rather than recognize the need. This may result in the dog feeling 'unheard', in turn intensifying the behaviour out of frustration. If the dog is seeking connection but can only elicit anger from the human, they may eventually settle for negative attention.

Nowhere had I seen this more pronounced than with my father's dog, Jeanu. My father used to keep the dog outdoors, which, in cities, leads to many behavioural problems. One of them is severe deprivation of human connection. It made Jeanu want to grab attention by any means possible. He had quickly come to learn that following the phrase 'NO, JEANU!', there would be a flurry of running behind him and fussing around him. That was good enough for him. He had systematically tried all things that elicited a 'NO, JEANU!' from us. If we were standing outside, he would jump up and grab our hair ties, run with them, and eat them up! Apart from hair ties, Jeanu had learnt to grab and swallow just about anything he could find, especially when he had people around him who would see him do it and run after him yelling and screaming.

One day, he managed to get into the house. While my sister and father chased him around, he ran up to my room, grabbed hold of the soft velvet belt that went around my robe and ate it! Guess what? That which goes in must come out. Every dog book needs at least one poop story, and here's mine. Ready or not, here it comes! My sister and father had been walking him hours later, wondering how this was all going to go. Then, it happened. Jeanu started going round and round in circles, found the exact spot and orientation he needed, and began to poop. But soon he realized that he was in trouble. That robe belt was *not* coming out on its own. He started getting agitated, unable to poop. My sister and father looked at each other. They knew one of them had to do this. To this day, I don't know who did it and how they did it, but the belt was successfully extracted. But that's not the most ridiculous part of the story. After the event, my father and sister discussed if they just wanted to throw that belt away, or wash it and put it back. Thankfully, until I heard this story years later, I believed I had lost that belt—meaning, no washing and replacing happened. Phew!

What I learnt from Jeanu is that a dog's need for connection is so strong that they are willing to engage in the most bizarre behaviour to get it and even settle for connection that comes in the form of anger or frustration. That clearly indicates that we absolutely need to meet that need, but how do we do so while also communicating that a dog needs to find other ways of expressing their need? It has taken me a few years and several observations of street dogs to understand how adult dogs do communicate this to puppies. They use simple but extremely well-timed body language cues such as turning their head and body away, timing it so well as to almost anticipate when the puppy is about to jump or nip. This cue seems to deter puppies from jumping or nipping. They are also good at recognizing other body language cues of puppies meant to seek connection and social engagement. They respond to these quite quickly, taking away the opportunity for the puppy to jump or nip as a way of expressing the need.

Dogs do have other ways of 'asking' for things. They can do this by simply staring with their big, liquid eyes. Recent studies show that they even have extra muscles in their eyes to help them achieve these beseeching looks. Most pet parents are familiar with that look their dogs give when begging for table scraps—one that melts our hearts. Streeties give us similar looks outside bakeries and eateries. We know what this look means, and we get the message immediately. Both streeties and pet dogs show us that dogs know how to ask us with their eyes. So many of us are intimately familiar with that 'puppy dog look' that makes us feel willing to sell our souls to them. They do have very endearing ways of asking us, and as streeties demonstrate to us, this may even be a survival skill they have developed over time. The trouble with our pet dogs is that far too often, we are too busy to notice these cues and end up ignoring them. I have had to remind clients to respond to a dog asking that way, and not let it escalate to having to jump, nip, bark or what their equivalent of 'shouting' may be.

Once I understood all of this, I decided to try it with my father's dogs, Puma and Buttons. These were two big dogs who were such intense jumpers that every time I went to his house, I had to write off the shirt I was wearing, which would get torn because of their nails getting caught in them or me falling on the floor. So I prepared myself. I stuffed an old backpack with towels, put it on my back, to protect my shirt and the skin on my back from getting torn and turned around. I used the wall to ensure that I didn't fall on my face. By turning away, I was hoping to emulate what the adult dogs were doing, as a way of telling them that I did not appreciate being jumped on, and sure enough, they got down for a second. As soon as they did, I also met their need for connection, by petting them calmly, showing them that they did not need to 'shout'. I did have to repeat this a few times, but eventually, they got the message. The backpack idea worked!

Once I managed to get Puma and Buttons to stop jumping on me, I decided to try to get them to stop jumping on Uttam. I guided him step by step through the whole exercise. Everything went well. Uttam turned away. The dogs got down immediately. I asked Uttam to pet them at this point, and that's when it stopped working. They were back and jumping like maniacs. I realized that it was because the second I asked Uttam to pet the dogs, Uttam got all hyper, rough-playing with them and saying, 'Who's a good boy, huh?' Obviously, they found it impossible not to jump. I had to request Uttam to keep calm, at least for a week, until the dogs understood that their jumping was not being appreciated. Some dogs will also need a specific type of touch, a kneading kind of action on their neck, which I suspect may have something to do with how they integrate tactile sensory input. Some dogs process touch a bit differently, and the 'wrong' kind of touch can get them agitated to the point of them jumping or nipping. In these cases, I simply try different things until I discover what has the most calming impact on that specific dog. For Buttons, it happened to be scratches on the rump; for Puma, it was a kneading action on the neck.

After successfully getting Puma and Buttons to stop jumping on Uttam, I decided to instruct my students on how to do this with their dogs. It worked in some cases, but failed in a few. In cases where it failed, I gathered videos to analyse it further. A few students were not timing their communication well enough, waiting too long to let the dog know that the jumping was not appreciated and by the time they got around to doing so, the dogs had worked themselves up too much. Interestingly, in all cases where the timing of the communication was good, the dogs were responding really well. All the dogs stopped jumping for a second or two. But in some cases the students just forgot to then meet the connection need of the dog or were too slow in doing so, frustrating the dogs and getting them to jump up again. Timing of the communication and identifying the specific need of the dog and meeting it rapidly was critical to getting dogs to stop jumping on people.

As you can see, there is no single solution that works for all dogs. It requires asking several questions as to why a dog is doing what they are doing, what needs of theirs they are trying to have met, how else we could consider meeting it, and what challenges they are up against. In some cases, it is also about our relationship with the dog, the state of mind they are in, and the timing.

Fortunately, I got an opportunity to watch Turid Rugaas demonstrate this when I was in Asheville in 2014. I had been studying with Turid that year. A lady called Grace was hosting Turid and me in her home. Grace had a Husky called Sesi, and it was clear that Sesi was not going to spare anyone her jumping. She didn't just jump, she would bounce several feet into the air, grab my hair and then dangle off it! She was one of the most intense jumpers I have ever come across. I have very curly hair, and one time, Sesi's teeth got stuck in my hair! How many people get to say, 'I once had a Husky in my hair.'?

So, when Grace suggested one morning that she wanted to bring out Sesi, I was very eager to watch how Turid was going to handle her. Turid was over seventy-five at the time, and I knew she was in no position to use strength to withstand a Husky jumping on her. No backpacks and no wall to lean against. There was no time to train Sesi. I knew this was going to be a learning moment for me. As Sesi raced towards us, I saw that Turid did not wait for her to jump. She saw the jump coming from a distance, flashed a quick hand signal to Sesi and then turned around. I repeated the same. Sesi just ran in a wide arc around us. It was the first time since I had been at Grace's that Sesi had not hung on to my hair. Observing Turid taught me about the elegance of good timing.

When I teach my clients how to get their dogs to stop jumping, I refer to all of this as part of a 'technique'. But what it really is, as Turid demonstrated to me, is a very elegant language. If practised and well-delivered, it is as effective, if not more, than any language you and I use. However, just like communication in all human languages, if I don't listen (observe the dog and get the dog's perspective), then communication can fail. How many times have we heard of one person in a relationship feeling 'unheard' and resorting to shouting? I have found that in many cases, when dogs offer us strange behaviour, it is a response to not being heard or understood.

There is, of course, one last factor to consider. For communication to work, the dog needs to do some serious listening and thinking too. They must be in the right frame of mind to be able to listen and process this information. A stressed, excited or hyperactive dog is unlikely to be able to either listen or learn anything. That is not very different from us. We too struggle to concentrate if we are too excited or flustered.

Unfortunately, many urban dogs are very hyperactive due to their lifestyle. With my clients, I closely examine their lives to find sources of excitement and stress to get them to eliminate or minimize their impact on their dogs. In this book, I repeatedly revisit the topic of urban lifestyles stressing dogs, because that really is my biggest takeaway from it all— that we are all leading incredibly excitable and stressed-out lives and, in turn, doing the same to our dogs. This pace, it would seem, is not meant for them, and many are unable to cope, resulting in what we call 'problem behaviours'. On the surface of it, a street dog's life may be more stressed than a pet dog's, but closer examination suggests that is not always the case. This lifestyle issue would perhaps also explain many of the behavioural differences between streeties and our pet dogs and deserves a much closer examination.

Destruction

Destruction was never really an issue for us with Nishi, since she was not much of a destroyer. She was once visited by two little girls in the apartment, who wanted to gift her a blue teddy. Years later, the teddy remained intact, each eye and ear in place—only the blue had become a distinct brown. Nishi has never been destructive and takes special care of her toys. In fact, the condition of her toys has made her somewhat popular at pet shops.

Tiggy, our second one, put me up against all the challenges Nishi did not, and none of the challenges Nishi did. Initially, Tiggy destroyed things quite a bit. Tiggy had a terrible past. Given her past and her nature, she is a skittish dog and gets anxious easily. When she does, she chews and destroys things.

Apart from anxious dogs like Tiggy, there is another category of dogs that frequently destroys things—hyperactive dogs. Why do they do it? What do excited dogs, anxious dogs and hyperactive dogs have in common? Elevated adrenaline and cortisol. Therein perhaps lies the answer. Studies on both humans and rats reveal that the chewing action increases endorphins and reduces cortisol. Thus, chewing helps them calm themselves down. Given this understanding of the function of chewing, I stopped viewing it as a problem and actually saw it as a solution. If I could get the dogs to chew on more appropriate things, I could get hyperactive dogs to calm down. It could also serve as a 'stress meter', telling me when a dog is getting too excited or anxious and needs a way to cope. It helps me examine lifestyles and find out the exact stressors in a dog's life.

At this point of the discussion with clients, a few point out that their dog has been given chew toys but are not chewing on that. I read an article that uses very fancy terminology to explain what we have all experienced as a dog's loss of interest in toys: 'an intense but transient neophilia towards novel objects'. Basically, dogs get bored easily. Personally, I use certain natural bones and dehydrated tendons. Other options such as green fibrous coconut husk or jute/coir rope pieces knotted and flavoured in different ways might also work. Failing to give the dogs appropriate things to chew on may result in them chewing more dangerous things and put them at grave risk. Animals chew for a reason, and that function must be met.

A few words of caution if you decide to offer bones to your dogs. Never give them thin bones that splinter easily or hard bones that can crack their teeth. We are looking for bones that encourage gnawing. Don't ever put yourself in a position to take a bone away from a dog. If you have multiple dogs, always offer them bones separately. Do not let the bone literally become the bone of contention. Further, always give bones under supervision and preferably with guidance from relevant professionals.

Eating Junk

Since Nishi never destroyed things, she never ate any of it. Of course, there were the early days of eating the bulletin board pin and mango seed. But those were just our early mistakes of interrupting her exploration sessions. As she got older, she got smarter and there was no junk eating. Tiggy did destroy things but never ate them. Phew!

I do, however, get a lot of clients whose dogs eat a lot of rubbish. This is often dismissed prematurely as pica. Pica is an eating disorder that may be caused by a nutritional deficiency or mental health conditions such as schizophrenia or obsessive compulsive disorder (OCD). But before we jump to such an extreme condition, we need to take a step back and ask if there is a simpler explanation. Do you remember our earlier discussion on streeties not eating plastic? That brings us straight back to the now-familiar question of whether we are doing something with our dogs that makes them eat plastic, and I am inclined to believe that we do. The answer came to me when one of my teachers, Anne Lill Kvam, narrated the story of a monkey that lived with her during her time in Angola. The monkey frequently walked on her desk, examining things kept there. One day, she noticed him examining her precious medicines that were hard to find and she gasped. That was enough to make him realize that the pills were special, and from then on, those pills were of utmost interest to the monkey. A monkey has no interest in bitter objects in a plastic box. But her reaction made them valuable to him.

Puppies start out by examining things to satisfy their curiosity. They don't have thumbs, so they must pick up things with their mouth. Then—we react! Our reaction suggests to the puppy the object is valuable. The puppy runs away with the object, to examine this seemingly valuable object in a corner, but we don't let the pup figure it out. Instead, we follow the pup and insist they drop the object. The pup feels cornered and might see no other option but to eat it. The more this cycle repeats, the faster the pup goes from exploring to eating it up.

In all of my work, there was one specific client whose dog was so extreme in this regard that when he was exploring something, if you so much as looked in his direction, he would grab the object, bolt to another room and quickly gobble it up. This client was also the most vocal when it came to reacting to her dog when he so much as sniffed something. Through the years, I've noticed that there is a high correlation between the intensity of a human's reaction and the dog's speed of going from exploring to eating rubbish. Of course, you remember my own story of Jeanu. Needless to say, my reactions were rather epic back then!

So, how do we get ourselves not to react? That's where it comes down to how aware we are and how ingenious we can get. The first step would be to puppy-proof. Then, give the dog access to different objects. At first, these can be things that would not be harmful if the dog ingested in small quantities. It is meant to be an opportunity for you to demonstrate to the dog that the object will not get snatched away. Introduce new objects, so that the dog has many occasions to get the message that you do NOT intend to take objects away from him. Note that dog toys may not work in this context. This is about gradually getting your dog to not get overly excited about your everyday objects. So, you need everyday objects and not toys.

One lady heard my explanation and decided to deal with her dogs who had a fascination for gobbling up paper cups. She brought home several organic paper cups, offered them all up to the dog and swore not to react. The dog gobbled up the first paper cup and looked at her. No reaction! He tore up the second and looked at her. She was still not reacting. His enthusiasm waned. He shredded another one, saw that there was nothing that was going to happen and stopped it all together. The problem went away in minutes and only one paper cup had been consumed, which easily passed in the poop. There! Another poop story and now we are truly 'talking dog'.

Bad Judgement in Dogs

Eating inedible things seems to be very poor judgement on the dog's part. In fact, many pet dogs seem to have rather poor judgement in general. I was once watching a webinar by a behaviourist who showed a picture of her dogs standing on top of a high structure without a ledge and looking down. Very few of us would trust our dogs to have the good sense to not jump. She, however, claimed that her dogs were calm enough to think through this and not make bad decisions. That immediately piqued my interest, because I can see that calm street dogs would very rarely take stupid decisions like jumping off tall buildings or eating inedible dangerous things like plastic. The more hyperactive pet dogs are, the less likely they seem to make wise decisions.

A dog that is not hyperactive is able to make good decisions and learns fast. It gets easier for them to learn not to jump on us or destroy things. A dog that is not hyperactive is also likely to pull less, walk slower, exploring more deliberately. A slow walk makes it easier to predict when things might go wrong and gives us more time to react. It seems that most so-called 'behavioural problems' vanish if the dog is calmed down. In my practice, this seems to be the single most effective tool for almost all problem behaviours, and I have come to see the value in focusing first on calming dogs down, before addressing any other behaviour. Once the dog is calm enough, there are often no more issues left to address.

Unfortunately, some people push back on the idea of calming a hyperactive dog. They feel that their dog is just being 'over-the-top happy' or is 'having a lot of fun', and they don't really want to change that aspect of their dog or see their dog less happy. However, happiness and hyperactivity are functions of relatively different sets of hormones, so a calm dog is not necessarily an unhappy dog. A calm dog is just as capable of experiencing the full extent of joy from things that make a typical dog happy. But being hyperactive comes at a cost, the details of which I dive into in the next essay.

HYPERACTIVE DOGS

The biology of behaviour starts in the brain, which orchestrates everything in the body through electrical signals and chemicals. When we get excited or anxious, the brain switches gears, from its rest and digest mode to a more active mode ready for action. This switch in technical terms is called the Sympathetic Nervous System Activation or SNS Activation. SNS Activation is coupled with high circulating levels of a chemical mix of adrenaline, noradrenaline, cortisol, osteocalcin, glucose and other chemicals. Together, these chemicals prepare the body for action. The exact role and long-term impact of these are still being understood, and for this discussion, I will simplify it and stick to just two of the chemicals: **adrenaline**, a hormone as well as a neurotransmitter, and **cortisol**, a naturally occurring steroid.

In humans, SNS Activation is somewhat easy to spot through actions such as biting nails, pacing, fidgeting, tapping of the feet and talking very fast. While different individuals may, out of habit, have different telltale signs of SNS Activation, there is an underlying commonality to all of it—a certain business to the above actions. SNS Activation works very similarly in most animals, including our dogs. Consider how dogs express excitement. Boxers may typically jump when excited, whereas Retrievers may choose to pick up things with their mouth. Beagles may howl, Shih Tzus may bark, and our own local mixed breeds may prefer to chew or rip things up. Several dogs run around in wild circles. Some dogs hump objects they see around them, while some pee. Different dogs respond to hormonal changes differently based on breed, health, habits and the personality of the dog. However, it's easy to spot behaviours that are associated with SNS Activation. There is the unmissable 'busy-ness' and frenzy in all these behaviours.

Before we proceed, it is important to emphasize that SNS Activation can be a result of excitement or anxiety. Its trigger is called a 'stressor', and this terminology is often misleading, conjuring up images of unpleasant triggers. However, we must not forget that excitement too increases adrenaline and has the similar physiological impact on the body as anxiety. An extreme example of this would be someone dying of a heart attack because they won the lottery. This is a classic case of extreme SNS Activation. Such an extreme activation could be a result of a massive scare or even extreme excitement. The body does not differentiate much, and neither do I for the purpose of this discussion. In fact, in the context of our dogs, excitement is perhaps the biggest contributor to repeated SNS Activation, and it's important to keep that at the back of our minds as we explore this topic.

The other thing to remember about SNS Activation is the toll it takes on the body. This is a powerful system in the body that turns on very rapidly, and the body takes a while to return to normal. It was designed this way because it was meant to be used rather sparingly in extreme situations. In his book *Why Zebras Don't Get Ulcers*, Robert M. Sapolsky discusses the idea of how our modern-day urban lives entail the constant turning on of this powerful system, with too little time between triggers, not giving the body a chance to recover fully.

Not allowing the body to return to normal can cause a build-up of hormones such as cortisol and keep the body in a high state of arousal, which can have far-reaching consequences on physical and mental health. The impact of chronic repeated SNS Activation is well-documented. Here is a brief overview for you:

1. **Heart**: This is perhaps the easiest to understand. We all know that both excitement and anxiety increase the heart rate. It's simply the body's way of pumping more blood rapidly to the muscles, getting them ready for action. But we also know that sustained high heart rates could lead to conditions such as atherosclerotic plaque, and sudden massive spikes could result in a cardiac arrest.

2. **Digestion**: You've perhaps experienced this phenomenon as the feeling of butterflies in our stomach or nausea. The hallmark of SNS Activation is moving the body out of 'rest and digest' mode. Blood supply to the digestive system is cut off, redirecting blood to the muscles. The result of sustained change of this nature includes reduced energy storage, reduced growth and, more directly, ulcers. There are studies that show that show-dogs and dogs that participate in sports have higher occurrences of ulcers, perhaps explained by this phenomenon.

3. **Excretion**: SNS has a dual impact on excretory functions. The body ceases digestion, thus ceasing the production of poop as well as pee, possibly resulting in constipation. At the same time, it may dump out the excess pee and poop already in the system. This may be experienced as diarrhoea, or a need to pee excessively. In dogs, peeing takes

an interesting form, given that their bladders are designed to store pee for communication. So, there's a lot more of the 'dumping' of the pee. This is very evident when we observe them in an environment that they perceive to be exciting or stressful. Some dogs will pee non-stop while some are just unable to pee or poop the whole time they are out of their home.

4. **Immunity**: In his book, Sapolsky provides a very detailed connection between high circulating levels of glucocorticoids and the gradual unwinding of the immunity of the body. This results in repeated allergies, infections and other lifestyle diseases, including cancers. Incidentally, we are beginning to see an upsurge of cancer in pet dogs as well, suggesting that our lifestyles are perhaps not sparing our dogs. On a less catastrophic level, it is not uncommon for dogs to have illnesses after stressful events like rehoming or chronic illnesses in cases of stressful or over-stimulated lives.

5. **Psychology**: Sustained exposure to excitement or anxiety not only results in the rewiring of thought processes and neural networks, but also makes the individual more sensitive to the triggers, which can lead to hyperexcitability, anxiety disorders, depression and other mental problems. Sadly, these mental problems are on

the rise in human populations as well as urban dog populations.

6. **Muscles**: Muscles tend to tense up when we are excited or stressed. This is a self-protection measure taken to protect oneself from injury. However, when muscles remain in that state for a prolonged period, they can result in different kinds of aches and pains all over the body. Ironically, this protective mechanism makes the muscles more vulnerable to injury and fatigue.

7. **Hormones**: Cortisol has a profound effect on the endocrine system of the body, which produces several hormones. Important hormones such as the thyroid hormone and insulin are part of this system, and if their production is impacted, it can cause irreversible damage to the body, which results in other lifestyle diseases like hypothyroidism and diabetes. In fact, the thyroid gland is known to be impacted by something known as adrenal fatigue. Incidentally, hypothyroidism seems to be on the rise at an alarming rate in modern-day pet dogs.

8. **Weight**: Many people feel that they have an unhealthy relationship with food, where they either overeat or under-eat as a result of stress. This is not just a feeling, but actual biology. Stress can result in people getting hypophagic and under-eating, or getting hyperphagic and over-eating. In addition, cortisol has an impact on

how the body stores calories. We are not strangers to this concept since many of us who deal with sustained stress also deal with weight gain and struggle to lose weight in a healthy way. Obesity is yet another lifestyle problem common in pet dogs.

9. **Injury**: If you've ever been in an accident or a fight, you know that often, the full extent of your injuries only emerges after the effect of adrenaline starts wearing off. Sapolsky explains this powerful pain-numbing effect of adrenaline by citing the example of a zebra that may be slit open during a hunt and yet continues to run, as if not impacted by the injury at all. Now, consider the impact of something this powerful on our dogs that engage in several physical activities. If they are hyperactive, they are likely to either not get signals from their body that certain actions can cause injury or are very likely to engage in movement that their normal instincts would have forbidden them from doing.

10. **Learning**: The dictionary defines learning as 'the acquisition of knowledge or skill through study, experience and/or from being taught'. Learning becomes complete when the knowledge or skill gained becomes stored as memory that can be retrieved or recalled at times of need. Adrenaline and cortisol interfere with both parts of this process: memory storage and recovery. Studies

show that high volumes of sustained long-term exposure to cortisol negatively impacts explicit memory as neural networks begin to shrink and no longer try to connect or form synapses. Moreover, sustained exposure can cause some parts of the brain (hippocampus) to suffer from glucocorticoid toxicity and start to degenerate.

We all experience some amount of excitement and stress in our lives. So do our dogs. All our bodies were designed to handle this to some extent. However, urban lives overload us with various positive and negative stimulation, to the point where our health and minds struggle to cope. In dogs, these manifest as behavioural problems and eventually unravel the body, just like in humans.

In the rest of this chapter, I will discuss how we can help our dogs calm down. However, I cannot overemphasize the need to minimize stressors in the first place. In the next few chapters, I explore further how we might be adding stressors to our dogs' lives. I invite you to examine your dog's life closely to see what may be contributing to excessive excitement or anxiety, and which of these can be avoided. While it may fill us with joy to see our dogs bounding around with immense amounts of energy, we must be responsible about what is healthy for them in the long term.

Relax Dawg!

When we got Nishi, there was another dog in the apartment called Yoda. Yoda jumped on people a lot, and the lady who walked Yoda would often be heard screaming, 'Relax, Yoda! RELAX!' I am yet to see someone who calms down because they were *asked* to calm down. It does not work for people, and it does not work for dogs! In my experience, what does work is sniffing, chewing and thinking. They sound deceptively simple, but let's take a closer look, shall we?

- **Sniffing**: Pranayama, a branch of yoga, is built on the principle of controlling emotions through breathing. How many times have we seen people panicking being asked to take a deep breath? Slow exhalation slows down the heart rate. Recollect our earlier discussion on the Sympathetic Nervous System (SNS). The SNS influences several involuntary systems of the body, such as the heart and the digestive system. The respiratory system, however, is the only voluntary system that is influenced by the SNS, meaning it is the only system that we can consciously control. We cannot make the heart beat slower, but we can slow down our breathing, which in turn, can reduce the SNS Activation in the body and indirectly slow our heart rate. In other words, it's really the only way to force yourself to relax. This is why so many relaxation techniques have such a strong breathing component.

  How can we use this idea, given that it might be a bit hard to get a dog to do yoga? The good news is that a dog is a creature of their nose, and we could use this to our advantage. A dog loves to use their nose, and it should really be easy to get them to sniff. Studies show that sniffing reduces a dog's heart rate. One of the most powerful ways is to take them on what we call a sniffing expedition or a 'sniffari'. It could be an empty plot, a construction site, a parking lot at odd hours. It does not have to be elaborate, simply interesting, with some peace and quiet for them to concentrate on the various odours that dogs typically find interesting—another dog's pee (we call this pee-mail), humans having walked, other animals, etc. I also get my dogs objects from outdoors that have interesting odours. It could be branches, pods or stones. If I visit other people's homes, I bring back something, especially if they have animals. I sometimes play nose games and searching games. Anne Lil l Kvam's book *The Canine Kingdom of Scent* outlines many nose games that can be fun for the dog.

On a sniffari in a country like India, which overloads the senses, dogs cannot handle more than fifteen to twenty minutes of such intense sniffing, just as it is hard to do Pranayama for too long. Sniffing is a powerful tool for humans and more so for dogs. Their sense of smell is anywhere between a few hundred thousand times to a few million times better than ours and their brains light up like a Christmas tree when they are sniffing. Use this tool wisely.

- **Chewing**: The second trick for calming a dog down is getting them to gnaw on or chew something. We already discussed earlier that when an animal is stressed, they chew. (So do humans. Think of people who chew on pens and pencils.) I have noticed that many dogs automatically use this coping strategy, chewing on objects when things get a bit too exciting or stressful. When I start work with a dog, I recommend that they use this tool a lot, because we notice that after a chewing session of about fifteen minutes or so, dogs doze off for almost two hours. We jokingly call this 'bone coma'. In the case of dogs that are quite calm in general, I use this more on days I notice them getting too excited or agitated.

- **Thinking**: We all know that if we are panicking, we cannot think, but did you also know that if you found a way to think rationally and mindfully, then it can help reduce the panic? The two don't mix! Therapists use this trick to help people deal with anxiety, asking them to try to make lists when they feel their anxiety rising. Studies show writing to be an effective tool to reduce stress and deal with stressful events.

  Can training dogs to do tricks gets them to think? Not always! Getting them to do repetitive tasks can get them to shut off the thinking part of their brain and can get them far too excited about the rewards involved. Training also entails constant interaction between humans and dogs, which also can get dogs quite excited. What dogs really need is quiet time to do some thinking and problem-solving on their own. Exploring, searching, figuring out how to get food out of containers—these are typically the kind of thinking street dogs seem to do. It's also easy to notice that if there is a lot of human presence, street dogs do not think as intensively. They either run away or engage with the human instead. Engagement with humans gets them excited, not calmer. So, while we try to simulate some of these scenarios at home for our pet dogs, to engage their minds, it is also important to find a way for us to disengage during this period and create an environment conducive for quiet concentration.

Dog Mentors

> *People can never raise perfect dogs.*
> *Only dogs can raise perfect dogs.*
>   —Turid Rugaas

I use the term 'pet parents' liberally in this book, because I do not like the idea of pet *ownership*, and the word *guardian* just does not capture the emotional connection. However, we do need to be aware that when we bring in a dog, we have in our homes a member of another species. Contact with their own species is important for their growth. Repeated observation of street dogs tells me that as much as we try to teach our pet dogs how to be polite, there is no replacement to a dog mentoring a dog. The mentor needs to be carefully hand-picked, and they need to enjoy mentoring. Moreover, the puppy should be open to being mentored by them. A good mentor–mentee pair should be like a good couple: the chemistry should be obvious.

Once you have determined that you have due consent from the mentor and pup, meet for a short duration, in a neutral territory. Don't let the first meeting be more than, say, fifteen minutes. I'd keep it at five, if possible, so that I end on a good note. Ending on a good note is far more important than making that first session long, so keep it as short as needed.

Dogs do not have to spend all their time rough-housing and playing with each other. While 'play' is important, other calm interactions such as exploring together are equally so. These can rarely happen in large group settings, where dogs can work themselves up into a frenzy. Mentorship is a meaningful interaction that needs space and time. It's also important to avoid interfering or influencing the interaction. Try to stay out of it as much as possible. Many of us push puppies towards non-stop play, which can get the puppy very hyperactive very quickly. A puppy needs to learn several social skills, playing being just one of them. A dog's social life is far richer than mindless play. A good mentor should be able to regulate play, end it when it is time, and transition into other kinds of lessons. If they cannot, then you need a better mentor.

Not all dogs are cut out to be mentors. Typically, teenage dogs do not make for great mentors; in fact, they teach more bad habits than good ones. Best to let teens be teens. Dogs that are too old also don't always have the patience or the energy for such work. A two-year age gap between the mentor and the mentee is ideal. Pick the mentor well, and then let them teach your dog the ways of the dog world.

The Dominance Myth

As we reach the end of this chapter, you will notice that nowhere in the entire chapter do I advocate dominating the dog or warn of behaviours that might lead the dog to believe they are the alpha. The concept of using dominance to get a dog to fall in line is now considered an outdated one that does more damage than good. The idea first came from studies that were done on captive wolves. It was observed that unrelated captive wolves seem to organize themselves in a linear hierarchy. This was then co-opted by dog trainers, who seem to have used it to justify harsh methods of training dogs.

However, newer ethological studies on both dogs and wolves paint a very different picture. Wolves in the wild do not seem to organize themselves like the captive wolves did, much like how human social behaviour in prisons is not a representation of human behaviours in wholesome families. More interestingly, free-ranging dogs have a social structure that is nothing like that of a wolf. I explain this in much more depth in the chapter titled 'Lives of Streeties'.

Apart from the invalidity of the idea that a dog is constantly trying to take over a household as the 'leader', requiring them to be shown 'their place' repeatedly, studies also show us that punishments, anger, irritation, intimidation have dire consequences on a dog's behaviour, physical health and the human's relationship with them. The concept of 'spare the rod and spoil the child' is considered outdated in human parenting today and it is the same when it comes to caring for animals. We simply don't need such methods. A quick search online on the 'dominance myth' will uncover plenty of material that shows that this tough approach is not only non-scientific, but also physically and mentally damaging.

When I got Nishi, I was clear that I was not willing to find myself in a place where I am in a power struggle with my dog, and Uttam was clear that he was simply not willing to get tough on Nishi. So, despite what we were told by popular media, we rejected the idea of trying to dominate her, and it was a huge relief to learn that we never needed to. My story, the one I want to share with you, is not of how I dominated my dog into submission, but of how I discovered and cherished the best in my dogs.

CHAPTER 3

THE BOARDING THAT NEVER HAPPENED

Of Summer Camps and Rave Parties

A few months after getting Nishi, we realized that we would have to travel soon and had to figure out how to board her. I enlisted the help of my sister, Shringar. Shringar and Nishi were great friends, and we had spent several evenings at my sister's house. It seemed that it would be easy enough for Nishi to start doing sleepovers at Shringar's. However, while she always welcomed Nishi with open arms, Nishi's excessive energy got to her at times. She would return her and exclaim, 'Okay, I can't keep up with this pup. I don't want her back here.' A few weeks later, she was all ready to take her back in again.

After having done a few sleepovers with Shringar, we were ready to try out boarding for real. We scouted all the options available. We visited all the ones we shortlisted. We asked a million questions. We interviewed the boarding staff intently. We visited them at different times of the day to see how things changed during the day. We checked on the nearest vet available. We asked if they had the luxury of a vet visit in the case of an emergency during odd hours. Nishi was the centre of our world, and we were unabashed about it.

After having picked her mentors so carefully, it would make just no sense to leave her with a pack of boarders at a boarding facility, with no supervision. We were very particular about what kinds of dogs she spent time with during boarding and how much time she spent with them. Being in a new environment is either too exciting or too stressful. In addition, there would be all these other dogs, often breaking out into a barking symphony. How easy would it be for a puppy to get sufficient sleep? Five days of vacation for us could mean five days of sleep deprivation for Nishi. In that environment, if a dog were to inappropriately approach another dog, could it possibly lead to one of the dogs snapping? Our primary criterion when boarding Nishi was her safety. We had to be sure that we came back to a safe, unscathed pup—albeit a slightly bored one.

When I talk to clients, they often view dog boarding as summer camps. Back then, I did too. In fact, I believe I once wrote an article where I described it exactly like that. The 'summer camp' image in our minds is the one that enables us to write off fights as 'children fighting'. But I have since come to realize that the 'summer camp' comparison trivializes the impact of such fights on dogs.

When fights break out between dogs, we need to take cognizance of it. Yes, there are little tiffs that happen between puppies, which is perhaps the equivalent of 'children fighting'. But when teenage or adult dogs are involved, it's an entirely different thing. Growling and snarling is not considered fighting, but posturing. From our own experience, this should ring true. While even the most belligerent of us might posture a lot, it takes a lot for us to throw a punch (at least, for the most of us). So when an adult of a species is involved in a physical fight, it's really a big deal. It can cause some severe emotional trauma, much like what would happen to you and me if we were to get mugged and beaten up. Puppies that get bullied might develop fear issues. Incidentally, puppies and teenagers that manage to bully others might learn how to become bullies for life. These are serious considerations when setting up a dog for a life of healthy social interactions.

Socialization is important for a dog to learn social skills. However, the environment must be conducive to learning. A frenzied environment is not the best, because it impedes rational learning. A rave party is not where one learns the nuances of good communication. Honing social skills happens with meaningful one-on-one interactions with a handful of individuals we care about. It happens with patience and under the guidance of nice adult animals, who are themselves experts in this skill.

Let me draw you a picture. A gorgeous lioness relaxing in the sun, humouring her little cubs and gently teaching them some early social skills. We don't see images in the wild of several unrelated animals of different ages, running around in a frenzy, learning to socialize. We don't see that among street dogs either. There is no concept of socializing with unknown dogs. In fact, we all know that trying to walk our dogs in a new territory means riling up all the street dogs there for several days, until they eventually make peace with your presence there, and, in a few cases, maybe befriend your dog. There are so many nuanced meet-and-greet behaviours and social interactions that first need to happen between these dogs, most of which remain unstudied and undocumented. When it comes to our pet dogs, though, we seem to want to write it all off. Even when we are dealing with adult dogs, we dismiss serious failure of social interaction as 'children fighting'. By doing so, we are not paying due attention and respect to the rich social lives of dogs.

FIGHTS AND AGGRESSION

Violence and *aggression* are somewhat different. Violence could be defined as a harmful social interaction, undertaken with the intention of inflicting harm or unpleasantness on another individual or individuals, or in retaliation, when provoked. Aggression, on the other hand, is an imitation of violence undertaken to *prevent* the situation from escalating to one of actual violence.

It includes a lot of posturing, meant to scare away the perceived threat.

Real violence is very rare in animals because the cost of violence is very high and the yield often too low. So, if there is a peaceful way to achieve something, a species will tend to gravitate towards this path. The only exception is perhaps hunting. For predatory animals, this is their only source of food, so violence cannot be avoided. The cost to the predators, however, is so high that they hunt sparingly and wisely. The oft-heard phrase 'animals don't hunt for sport' is true because real violence is very expensive. Animals such as dogs, who can rely on strategies other than hunting, do so preferentially. Dogs voluntarily opt for other 'cheaper' options, such as scavenging and begging. Animals in general are frugal when it comes to spending their energy, since it is critical for survival.

Violence can be premeditated or impulsive. While several of the crimes we witness in the human world have to do with premeditated violence, what we witness in the animal world is more impulsive. The human penchant for premeditated violence might explain why humans tend to misinterpret animal violence as premeditated too. The problem with such an interpretation of their actions is that humans tend to respond to violence with violence. In reality, animals hate violence and do whatever they can to avoid it, which can be seen by the large repertoire of distance-creating signals that are meant for a lot of posturing. When a dog does bite, it was unavoidable from the dog's point of view. We need to acknowledge this for us to be able to ask ourselves what made aggression and its escalation to violence unavoidable to the dog. To be able to effectively answer this, we need to know what triggers aggression in animals. So, let's dive deeper into aggression.

1. **Fear** often is one of the biggest reasons for aggression. Fear creates a massive stress response in the body, triggering the 'fight or flight' response. Whether the animal chooses to fight or to flee could be based on the history of the organism, the health of the animal, genetics and the animal's perceived options to flee. Most times, dogs that show aggression are afraid of getting hurt, either due to the anticipation of malicious actions or as the unintentional result of interaction when a dog is already uncomfortable or in pain. So, more often than not, this is a defensive reaction.

2. **Frustration** also has a way of resulting in aggression and/or violence by triggering the rage system. Things that typically lead to frustration in animals could be confinement or being prevented from engaging in functional behaviours that help them cope with stressors. Irritation can trigger the rage system too. Dogs that are in chronic pain or constantly kept in

an over-stimulating environment are easily susceptible to irritation due to high levels of residual cortisol. In humans, one can understand this as 'frayed nerves', and it is easy to see how people with frayed nerves are quick to get angry or react badly.

3. **Resource guarding** can also trigger aggression in animals. Animals have to fend for themselves, and having resources is key for survival. Most animals learn how to share these resources in order to survive and don't really need to fight for them. However, the rules of sharing in animal societies are quite nuanced, subtle and include a lot of specialized communication. Currently, we don't have a good enough understanding of how dogs share resources. However, when dogs come to live in our homes, because of our limited understanding of these rules, we can often violate their rules of sharing or push animals to a point where they start to violate the rules among themselves. This can then make the animals feel like these survival resources are at risk, which in turn leads to food, space, people or object insecurity. Insecurity is always best dealt with by building security. Insecurity and fear are closely related and just like with fear, dogs need reassurance and freedom to work past their insecurities and build confidence.

4. Another kind of aggression, which is a lot more complicated than the others, is 'appetitive aggression'. In humans, this is seen in people with PTSD as a *coping mechanism*. It is not difficult to imagine that dogs who have been through severe trauma, and have successfully used aggression and violence in the past to protect themselves, can also be experiencing appetitive aggression. As one can imagine, this is not as simple to understand as the other types of aggression and usually develops in extreme conditions, making it difficult to overcome.

5. **Health issues** can also lead to aggression and, in many cases, even violence. Poor gut health, chronic pain and chemical imbalances in the brain are just some of the health conditions that can result in violent behaviours.

Now that we understand aggression a little better, let's take a look at some of the myths that revolve around aggression.

Myth 1: Eating meat causes aggression.

A common myth in India is that dogs who eat meat will develop a taste for it and might end up biting us. They are making the crucial mistake here of confusing the predatory hunting with aggression. A dog biting a human is not about them wanting to eat the human.

Dogs understand that we are important for their survival and well-being, and they do not view us as food. A meaty diet is actually quite species-appropriate for dogs and improves their overall health and mental well-being.

Myth 2: Neutering can cause/reduce aggression.

For a long time, it was believed that testosterone was the cause for inter-male aggressive behaviour and that castration would be the solution. However, studies today prove that aggression is more complex than that. Testosterone, like all hormones, does not directly influence aggression, only the expression of the behaviour. There is much more to aggression than inter-male aggression. In fact, in some cases, removal of testosterone can make the animal more fearful, which could lead to aggression. Animal Birth Control procedures are very important in a country like India, where we have a serious dog overpopulation problem. However, it should *not* be viewed as a solution for behavioural problems. The relationship between castration and behavioural changes is far more nuanced. Generalizations can be dangerous.

Myth 3: Aggression can be extinguished with exposure to the triggers and training.

Some people use punishments while others use rewards to extinguish aggression. People who try to punish what they perceive as bad behaviour may decide to either hurt or scare the animal displaying aggressive behaviour. This ends up overloading an already overactive 'fight or flight' response, which could escalate the aggression or push the animal to completely shut down. This is unfortunate, because the more we understand aggression, the more we know that it's rooted in something very unpleasant for the dog—a horrible past, a hidden pain, an unknown stressor or brain chemistry that the dog cannot help. This means that the dog is already going through something unsavoury. The question is, as loving pet parents, would we like to make it easier or more difficult on them?

The other approach to extinguishing aggression is to reward an alternative behaviour. Here too, we are only dealing with behaviour and discounting the underlying cause. For example, a dog displaying aggression towards another dog at home could be doing so because they are suffering from undiagnosed muscle injury or stiffness, and they might be afraid that indulging in play with the other dog in the house may lead to more pain. The dog might try to protect themselves by preventing the situation, by growling or showing aggression. Rewarding an alternative behaviour might extinguish the growling, but we might miss out on the underlying pain because the behaviour is now gone. Therefore, before we try to extinguish any kind of behaviour, it is important to acknowledge that the behaviour serves a certain purpose and examine what the underlying cause may be.

These are my top tips to help dogs displaying aggressive behaviour:

1. **Stop being angry** at such animals and opt for compassion and empathy.

2. **Identify the unintentional stressors** that may be present in a dog's life. This may include things like the animal being confined or crated (confinement is a big stressor for most animals due to loss of freedom), lots of commotion or stress in the home environment, activities that make the dog very hyperactive or put the dog on edge, and artificial pressure to keep resources safe (as can occur with multiple dogs eating in the same location). We then try to find ways to reduce or remove these stressors, and often, such simple changes can bring about the most dramatic results.

3. **Closely examine the dog**, looking for possible health issues. This includes things such as the way the dog moves, their posture, their appetite, food and water consumption (the choice of food that they want to consume and the composition of the food they are being fed), and the consistency and frequency of their poop and pee.

Dogs are not wired to bite us. We must understand and internalize this when we work with our dogs. We need to stop viewing aggression as an offensive behaviour and instead see it as a cry for help, which is what it really is. If we just slow down to see what really is ailing the animal, we are in the best place to bring about long-term meaningful change to the quality of the animal's life.

The Boarding that Never Happened

I am going to take you back to Nishi's story, which takes a sharp turn in 2011. By now, Nishi was all of eleven months. Uttam and I had both quit our corporate jobs and were looking for the next thing to do in our lives. It was also the wedding season in our family: three weddings and an engagement in a month. We had visitors flying in from all over the world for the season, and we knew it would be chaotic. One of those weddings was our own. Thanks to Nishi, our relationship had grown to a point where we were ready to get married.

Our wedding was to happen on Havelock islands in the Andamans. Uttam and I loved diving. Since we had both cut off our corporate ties, we were toying with the idea of moving to Havelock and becoming dive masters. 'Beach dog' would be a good avatar for Nishi. It seemed that we were at the brink of a lot of change and there was a lot of planning coming up. We needed to escape it all for a bit. We planned to go on a short trip to Nashik to clear our heads and plan the next phase of our lives.

We were supposed to leave the day after Uttam quit his job, first thing in the morning, but Nishi's boarding facility would not open until later in the day. So Nishi was to spend the previous night at my sister's and leave for boarding the next day—the boarding that never happened! The month was February. My birthday was coming up soon and this trip was supposed to be a birthday gift too. I suffer from travel anxiety, so I started fretting. 'I am supposed to spend my birthday with my little Nishi. Why are we going away? I hope the trip is cancelled. I wish something would make us drop out ...' I droned on and on. You know what they say about being careful what you wish for? Take my word for it. Be careful. Be very careful!

Uttam was tired of my mumbling, grumbling and sulking. He suggested that we take a walk with Nishi before we left for my sister's place. He hoped it would take my mind off my travel anxiety. 'We do one last walk with her, then, we pack, spend the night at your sister's and take off from there. What do you say?' That made sense to me. I did want to set free those butterflies in my stomach.

It's at this point that I need to take a deep breath. All this happened years before I started writing this book, but my gut still churns as I recall the events. My pulse races, and I can hear screaming in my head.

When we left for a walk, the traffic was nasty. We stood in a corner trying to cross the road. I held Nishi close. Just feeling the hot exhaust of the cars passing by was making me nervous. In a moment of respite, we quickly crossed the road and scurried to a lane. Offices were just winding down. Cabs filled this lane too. We continued to flank Nishi on either side, protecting her, and walked into a smaller lane. Relief!

This lane took me back decades. It reminded me of the times we played cricket and hopscotch on the streets. Children still did on this particular lane. There were cars of yesteryears parked by, the likes of Fiat Padminis and Maruti 800s. People let their dogs and children out on the streets and called them back in for meals. The lane was lined with trees to a point where the whole area had one giant shadow. People knew their neighbours by name and took out time to say hello. It sounds idyllic, does it not? Well, we thought so too. That's why we felt this was right for our Nishi. Still, we could never be too careful with Nishi, so we always walked her between us, protecting her from anything that might pose a threat. By now, I must sound a bit paranoid. Perhaps I was.

As soon as we entered the lane, Nishi got visibly excited. Up the road was one of her best friends, Mojo. Mojo, a strutting boxer, was a big fan of Nishi too. They eagerly awaited each of their encounters and their little game was utterly amusing. We loved to watch them interact. Uttam and I looked at each other, smiled and shook our heads. *Our eager beaver!* We doubled up and got to Mojo's house. Mojo was sitting on the porch, watching birds. Nishi stood at the gate and watched him for a while. Then she let out a little sigh. Mojo was still fixated on the birds, so she stuck her nose to the gate and let out a little yelp. He looked at Nishi and started wagging his butt with joy. He ran up to her. The instant his snout was close to hers, she turned away, walked a few feet away and looked away! What a tease! Mojo whined, yelped, cried and barked, but Nishi kept looking away. We laughed and suggested to Mojo that he put up his price too, but poor innocent Mojo just whined on. I know today that Nishi was just communicating to Mojo that this was going to be a non-confrontational, calm encounter, but to our untrained eye then, it looked quite comical. Nishi finally deigned to look at him, and they broke out in play. In typical boxer style, they both reared up and started punching each other. What a joy it is to watch two dogs play with such abandon!

Mojo's human, Vijay, walked out and towards us. We exchanged pleasantries. He opened the gate and let Mojo out. He suggested we let Nishi off the leash too. I grimaced. I hated letting Nishi off the leash, in fear of traffic, but Vijay had pointed out to me on several occasions that there were children and dogs playing on the road all the time and it was safe to do so. The road was so narrow that any driver would need to use utmost skill to just dodge past all the parked vintage cars, let alone speed past them. I did not want to sound like an obsessive pet-mom and saw the logic in his argument. I also have to admit, nothing gave me more joy than watching Nishi play.

I sighed and looked at Uttam. He gave me a nod of approval. Partly excited about her play, partly anxious about her safety, I took off her leash. The dogs burst into play, running around our feet and doing their odd doggy dance. Whenever we took Nishi off the leash on the road, we always stood on either end of the road, even if it was to stop bicycles and scooters. Nothing, absolutely nothing was to come close to harming Nishi. This time too, Uttam and I headed towards opposite ends of the roads to stand guard.

In movies, when something momentous happens, everything seems to happen in slow motion—every detail and sound slowed down and magnified and clear as crystal.

That's rubbish.

I don't know what happened next. I just stood still in the darkness that surrounded me. I could not see anything. I could not hear anything. Something inside me said, 'SCREAM, WOMAN! SCREAM!' I did not know how to. I did not know why I had to scream. Something was happening in my belly. Finally, the 'something' shot through me and emerged, and I heard it. It was a scream. From deep within me. No words, just a primitive guttural '*aaaaaaa*'. It was a cry. Then the sound stopped. Silence. I don't know how long it took me to snap out of this vortex I seemed to be in. It must have been less than a second but it felt like years, as if I had been transported from one universe to another parallel universe.

When I finally snapped out of it, I heard sounds, I saw things. I barely understood. What I did understand made me sick. I saw a car in front of me. I don't know where it had come from, but it was there. Exactly where the two dogs were frolicking just a few moments ago. The dogs were not to be seen. I heard a cry. An animal was crying. I saw people rushing around me. I thought I had started to understand, but I did not. All I could do was to let out another scream. *Where are the dogs? Where is my Nishi? Who is that animal that is crying? Make it stop crying. I need to concentrate. I need to look for my Nishi. Make that animal stop crying! STOP IT!*

Uttam was on the other side of the car. I walked up to him. I needed his help to find Nishi, but he was busy screaming at the driver of the car. What was wrong with him? Why was he not looking for Nishi? He was thumping his fist on the car bonnet and motioning the car to back up. 'Uttam! Nishi!' I said. I wanted him to stop doing whatever he was doing and help me find my baby girl, but I could not get his attention. The car backed up and Uttam slumped on the ground. What was wrong with him?

I looked down. I saw something that my brain refused to recognize. I kept asking myself, 'What is that? Where is Nishi?' That 'thing' that Uttam was now cradling was what had been crying. That 'thing' was a lump of black, and there was an eye staring into the sky. That 'thing' was … *no … how could that be?* My Nishi was full of life. She was full of joy. She lacked an ounce of sorrow in her life. She *was* joy. That 'thing' was not my Nishi.

'*Aaaaaaaaaaaaaaaaaaa!*' I screamed again and looked up at the sky. '*Do something, universe!*' my mind screamed. '*It was just a second ago. Reverse time. Just undo it.*' I looked at Uttam, and he was whispering to her, 'I love you. You are a good girl. We love you.' I heard loss in his voice. I looked around helplessly. Someone could do something for sure. Somebody! Help!

Suddenly, something happened. I looked down at Uttam, and we both knew. We knew we had to act. In that moment, we both knew that Nishi was not leaving us yet. 'Car! I need to get my car!' Vijay offered to drive us in his car. 'Where's Mojo? Find him,' I continued in my panic mode. Vijay reassured me that Mojo was perfectly fine, just a bit shook up. 'I need to get money,' I said. Vijay's father pulled out his wallet and handed me a wad of cash. We loaded Nishi in the car and headed out. By now, we had hit peak traffic hour. Uttam suggested that we not go to our regular vet, but to the closest vet. Off we went.

When we reached the vet, I jumped off the car and ran in, screaming, 'Help! Please help! My dog has been hit. Please help!' All the people at the vet's place were busy watching TV and looked at me at what seemed to me a tediously slow pace. They stared blankly at me. I ran out and no one ran behind me. I ran back in and pleaded again, 'Please help me. My dog has been hit!' Still no reaction. Just blank stares. I gave up and ran back to the car. Together, we brought Nishi into the vet's clinic.

By now, the people had been stirred into action. They had set up the table for her and helped us load her on to the table, but the vet was not in. The good doctor was stuck in the notorious Bangalore traffic and was an hour away. His assistant could not administer any strong medication in fear of her going into shock. So all we could now do was wait for an hour, giving her mild medication and watching her.

That's when it sunk in. This was my Nishi. She lay there, patiently, face torn apart and not a peep. Every few minutes she looked at us for reassurance. We were constantly on the phone with the vet. He asked us to check with Vijay if he could find any remains of her brains on the road. Feeling sick in my gut, I made that call and asked that question. 'Does not look like it, but I cannot tell. It's too hot and everything's melted.'

Great! More uncertainty and more waiting.

The vet finally arrived. Surgeries started on her. They went on for hours. I kept pleading with the vet to just tell me that Nishi would live. He refused to say it. I sat, shaking, at the vet's clinic and telling myself … well … what could I tell myself? Irrational demands to the universe to undo it? False hopes that she would be fine? What could I tell myself? *Are we running late to the airport? Oh wait, we are not going anywhere. What about her boarding? Oh wait, she is not going anywhere, is she? Is she going away from us forever? No. I should not think that way. Then what should I think?* I don't think my mind could hold on to a single cogent thought of any kind. We just waited, sobbing and holding each other's hands. Just with that action we said so much to each other—and yet, nothing useful. What could be useful at an hour like this?

Over the next few days, we gathered that Nishi was going to live. Still, it took us months to realize what a fighter she was and years to learn that she was not going to just live but thrive in the sheer joy of every moment life had gifted her.

The months to follow, however, tested us to the hilt. Surgeries became routine. Nishi was operated on countless times, X-rayed a dozen times, and she visited the vet almost every alternate day. It broke us down—physically and emotionally; we are still picking up the pieces today. Those were dark days, but they have taught us what we are made of.

Leash Aggression

Months after that fateful evening when we went on our first walk, we were back on that lane—the lane that I had once adored and which now made us uneasy. We walked past Mojo's house. Mojo saw Nishi from a distance and came running towards her. He stood at the gate and whimpered for her attention. And to our surprise, Nishi wanted to have nothing to do with him. She made a wide arc around his home and walked away. The next day, she seemed reluctant to enter the street. The day after, she flatly refused to go there. If she saw Mojo on another street, she walked away from him. We finally came to accept that Nishi was no longer friends with Mojo. She wanted to have nothing to do with him. We just accepted her rejection of his friendship and respected her need for distance. We did, however, wonder why she had severed her friendship with Mojo. What had he done?

This is where my education helped me understand my Nishi. Dogs often learn by association. That means if a dog is hurt while concentrating on another dog, they can develop a fear of the other dog. In this case, Nishi's attention was on Mojo when she was run over, so she developed a fear towards him. She showed no fear towards cars or drivers. In fact, to date she adores car rides. But she started avoiding Mojo. When she could not avoid him, she cried and wailed, and if that did not help, she growled and lunged. Think about the implication of this concept of associative learning. In the first chapter, I discuss how collars can cause pain. Imagine your dog is looking at another dog. Now, if you pull on the leash, fastened to a collar around the neck, they can associate the pain with the other dog. The next time they see another dog, they will anticipate the associated pain and want to either try to escape it or defend themselves (flight or fight). Noticing them tense up, you are likely to yank again. More pain. It might not take long for your dog to decide to take matters into their own hands and, at the very least, scare away the other dog that is 'causing' them so much pain. And that is often the birth of 'leash aggression'.

One of the more interesting complaints I get in class is that a particular dog is leash-aggressive only towards other dogs on leashes and not towards streeties. I sometimes get the opposite claim too: that the dog is aggressive only towards streeties and not towards pet dogs. When I dig a bit deeper, I often notice that the owner's anxiety towards these sets of dogs closely mirrors that of the dog. If the anxiety is the owner's, it's very likely the owner tends to tighten the leash when on edge. That explains the dog's behaviour.

I don't like the term 'aggression', because it becomes a self-fulfilling prophecy, where pet parents believe the dog is exhibiting offensive behaviour, which is then met with more punishments, training, disciplining, etc. As discussed in the essay on aggression, these tactics do not make the problem go away. They exacerbate it, or in extreme cases, the dog shuts down, becomes apathetic and even slips into depression. This often has a semblance of obedience. When I see a dog that exhibits none of the normal curiosity a healthy animal should, it gets me wondering. I see streeties, and I see normal curiosity and a fit mind. I see some of the 'obedient' pet dogs and I see a shutdown dog, whose spirit is broken. It really is important to understand fear for what it is. When we see fear or apathy in an animal, our desire is to protect them. As long as we don't make the error of mislabelling fear as aggression and apathy as obedience, we seem to know what the right thing is to do by the animal. That's why we need to pay attention to the labels we use.

The Nishi Spirit

Fear of Mojo was the emotional injury Nishi sustained from her accident. She also sustained several irreversible physical injuries. She gradually lost vision in her right eye. Her right nostril lost its moisture and ability to sniff. Saliva secretion ceased on the right side of her mouth. She lost several teeth on her right side. Her jaw was broken, and when it healed, it almost sealed her mouth shut. Her food has to be mulched up and she can eat only from her left side. Basically, the right side of her face has been destroyed. Since she has no control on that side, she drools profusely from it, far more than boxers normally do. When I see her drool, I jokingly call her *Julia Droolia*.

But Nishi's spirit shines through all of her injuries. To date, when I tell people she is blind on one side and can barely open her mouth, people find it hard to believe me. I need to point it out for them to notice. All they see is a spirited boxer who does not seem to know how to stop having fun.

One of the most touching stories of her spirit shining through has to do with her toys. Well, with her, most of her stories have to do with toys. During the year that followed the accident, Nishi was in and out of surgeries, and her face had to be kept in one of those cones, called an Elizabethan collar. We felt really sorry for our puppy, but she was done being sorry for herself. She saw the cone as a handy tool to carry her toys in. Often, we would find her with a toy in her mouth, and one or two toys tucked in her cone! She also used it as a way to avoid bumping her head into things on her blind side, while she dashed across the house, bouncing off the walls with her cone.

During the end of last year, I decided to gift all my clients and well-wishers some bookmarks. I got them printed and wanted to tie ribbons on all of them. I sat down, spread out my craft kit and started cutting out the ribbons. Nishi wanted to be a part of it. She asked if she could. Fearing that *Julia Droolia* would damage all my bookmarks, I refused. She would not give up. I am no less adamant. I would not budge. She parked herself in front of me, put on a mopey face and started letting out a little cry every few minutes. After a while, I let out an exasperated sigh and exclaimed, 'She just does not give up, does she? Stubborn dog!' Uttam turned around and said, 'You really think she should be giving up? Would she have been with us if she ever gave up through all that happened to her? What if she gave up back then?' That hit me like a ton of bricks. I apologized to Nishi, thanked her for attitude and never giving up. I invited her to check out my bookmarks. I had to throw a few away, but who cares? I had a puppy like Nishi in my life.

Talking to Dogs

That year taught us many lessons. We learnt how tough dogs really are, and their will to fight for life. We learnt about their willingness to forgive us. We learnt about fear. Most importantly, I learnt how to listen to dogs.

That February set me off on a quest that altered the course of my life. It brought into my life a lady I owe so much to—Turid Rugaas. From my current vantage point, I can safely say that when tragedy hit Nishi, I knew far too little about dogs. However, I had seen what trauma of this nature can do to dogs. First, all those visits to the vet during which she was cut open, poked and prodded were highly likely to make her very fearful of vets. Secondly, I had seen dogs having been through far less, developing massive behavioural changes, like becoming fearful or highly reactive, to the point of biting members at home. Lastly, I worried that having taken her to the vet so many times, putting her through so much pain, and pinning her down on the gurney so many times would make her lose her trust in us. If that happened, who in the world *could* she trust? What a scary place to be for a dog—living in a man-made world. Would we lose the Nishi we had? Would we even recognize the new Nishi? Would we have killed off that which made Nishi Nishi? Would I be left with only a shell of what once used to be a happy puppy? I started frantically looking around to see who could help me. I researched several experts around the world and reached out to all of them. A few responded. One made sense. The rest is history.

Turid introduced me to the idea of first trying to understand an animal that I am trying to help. How could I possibly understand what Nishi was going through? It's not like I could put her on a psychiatrist's chair and ask her to talk about her feelings. Or could I? The answer is not that simple. While I would not put her on any chair, I sure could ask her how she felt, and interestingly, even without having to ask, Nishi was telling me. I just did not know how to listen, until I ran into Turid.

Many people can instinctively see that dogs do express themselves. Most of us can see that dogs who are happy perhaps wag their tail while dogs that are afraid perhaps tuck their tail between their legs. Dog communication, however, is far richer and more nuanced than that. The last essay of this chapter focuses on dog communication and is really the first step to building a better relationship with our dogs. Like with most relationships, listening is a big part of it, and a big part of listening to an animal is knowing their language. That is where it all needs to start.

DOG COMMUNICATION

Communication is defined on Wikipedia as 'the act of conveying intended meaning from one entity or group to another, through the use of mutually understood signs and semiotic rules.' The question for us is: do animals communicate? They absolutely do. Not only do they communicate, but communication is also critical for survival in many cases. We can see how important communication really is based on how some animals have evolved to have elaborate physical characteristics and abilities that aid in effective communication—the beautiful plumage of a peacock, an animal's ability to emit and detect specific odours or frequencies, to change colours or build fascinating structures. The animal world is so replete with communication that there is an entire field of study dedicated to it: Biosemiotics, defined in Wikipedia as 'studies of the prelinguistic meaning-making or production and interpretation of signals in the biological realm'.

For social animals, not communicating is not even an option. They live in a very dynamic world with unpredictable situations that they must deal with, relying heavily on teamwork to procure food and defend themselves and care for their young. Team members do not have fixed, repetitive roles all the time. They need to be just as dynamic as the environment around them, and they need to quickly communicate with each other to be able to coordinate their actions. Social life essentially collapses without communication.

Human communication is characterized by our linguistic ability, which sets us apart from the rest of the animal kingdom. Dogs, it seems, are truly our best friends, in that they recognize this and try quite hard to cater to our 'special needs'. Compared to their wolf cousins, dog communication involves a lot more vocalization, just to get us to listen. Turid, in her book *Barking: The Sound of a Language*, identifies and differentiates seven different kinds of barks. Additionally, there are several sounds that dogs make that are yet to be effectively classified. Interestingly, studies also show that most human beings who have lived with dogs have the inherent ability to not only recognize many of these different vocalizations but also understand what they are meant to communicate.

Linguistics, however, remains a human dominion. While dogs try to include a significant vocal component in their communication with humans, the larger part of their repertoire comprises facial expressions and body language. This seems to be a gift from their ancestors and shared with their cousin canids. Imagine a pack of wolves—hunting, chasing after a large prey. Their prey will try to change its direction and do everything in its power to outrun them, so the pack needs to have a coordinated response to the movements of the prey. This happens through the exchange of subtle visual signals barely noticeable to the human eye.

Turid, in her book *On Talking Terms with Dogs: Calming Signals*, has documented about 30 such signals. I will not get into much detail about what these signals are because Turid's book does a very good job of it. However, I will discuss a bit about how to interpret them. We must recognize that what we are trying to do is to understand the language of dogs. We know that the best way to learn a new spoken language is not to try and translate the words, but to immerse ourselves in the language, to observe the context in which it is being used and try to understand what is being communicated. Turid classifies signals into two large contextual buckets: distance-creating signals and calming signals.

- **Distance-creating signals**: These are signals meant to ask for an *increase of distance*. Many animals have signals in this category. Consider the frill neck lizards flaring out their frill or the hiss of a snake or the growl of a tiger. They are all meant to say, 'Go away!' Our dogs, too, have a good collection of such signals, which include snarling, growling, lunging, showing of teeth, etc. These signals have something in common: they all look big and menacing because they are meant to scare away the threat and thereby meant to avoid conflicts. As discussed in my essay on aggression, violence is incredibly expensive on the body and most animals develop ways to avoid it.

  In the wild, when we see animals give us these signals, the communication seems to work. We seem to get what they are actually trying to tell us and we reciprocate with the right response. We don't really need a book or any other guide to tell us that these signals are asking us to create distance, and we back off. If we are in a situation where we have to approach these animals, say in the case of a rescue mission, then we tend to be very cautious and very reassuring about how we approach such an animal. We somehow seem to be aware the animal is feeling cornered and that is what is pushing them to have this defensive reaction towards us. However, at home with our dogs, the interpretation changes drastically. Growls and barks are often interpreted as offensive messages and are met with anger, aggression and need for 'behavioural corrections'.

When an animal gives out a distance-creating signal, what they are saying is, 'Please back off. I feel pushed and I feel like I might have to bite. I don't want to bite, so please back off.' It is critical for us to recognize distance-creating signals for what they are and respond appropriately. If we don't, the animal may feel pushed enough to resort to self-defence, and in the case of a dog, this is a bite! Of course, if a dog is giving out these signals too frequently, then it's a good idea to try to understand why they feel pushed so frequently. A professional might be able to help get to the bottom of the issue. Meanwhile, the only safe instantaneous response to a dog giving a distance-creating signal is to *create distance*.

- **Calming signals**: These are signals used in less extreme social interactions. They communicate ideas such as 'I come in peace'; 'I mean no harm'; 'Don't hurt me, please'; 'That's making me a bit nervous', etc. They all seem to communicate ideas of peace-brokering, to maintain harmony during social interactions. Hence, Turid calls them calming signals. Some of these signals are licking, tongue-flicking, sniffing the ground, turning away/turning of the head, walking slowly, sitting down, freezing, walking in a curve, yawning, lying down, splitting, 'smiling' and 'frozen play bow'.

Once I learnt about these signals and started to observe them, I suddenly felt like my dogs were being extremely chatty. Of course! Imagine a language with seven words (barking only) versus a language with thirty words (facial expressions and body language). However, what is fascinating is that it is not just dogs that use these signals. My colleagues, students and I have also observed these signals in other animals such as cows and cats. A recently published book documents these signals in horses. On one of my vacations to Sakleshpur, I saw Nishi and the resident horse, Jack, 'talking to each other' exchanging these signals. Watching it suddenly made me realize that many animals seem to be in on this and have some common denominator with which they are able to communicate with each other to some extent. Dogs are actually trying to rope us in by trying to use it a lot more on us than other animals do. Once I learnt how to read these signals, I suddenly felt like I had been invited to join in on this conversation.

This brings us to the next question. Can we only be passive listeners in these conversations, or can we 'speak' too? Is there an inherent two-way communication between humans and dogs? It should not be hard for us to imagine that there indeed is. Humans and dogs have been working as a team well before the age of training, 'keeping pets' or breeding; if team work relies on communication and if effective communication is necessarily two-way, then it stands to reason that we do know how to talk to our dogs without actually having to train for it. Turid taught us a few 'signals' of our own that my students and I have been trying on street dogs. We do not try to train them in any way but try to observe how many of our signals they can inherently understand. Our observations have blown our minds away and we are in the process of conducting formal studies to document them!

One such signal that Turid has documented is what she calls 'splitting'. If a dog is nervous about someone or something, you could stand between the dog and whatever is making the dog anxious with your back to the dog and your hands relaxed on your side, your open palms facing the dog. This seems to reassure the dog that you are taking charge of the situation and they do not have to feel nervous.

As I write this book, by my count, there are close to ten signals and gestures that remain undocumented but can be effectively used by people to communicate different things to dogs, including getting their attention, asking them to come to us, warning them not to approach, providing reassurance and drawing boundaries. Training a dog to learn English words is less fascinating to me. I am convinced by now that they have the ability to learn several words across multiple languages. Some dogs show the ability to chain words, some have been found to have a repertoire upward of a thousand words and the ability to learn novel words on their own. The more interesting question for me is how much of untrained communication we can recognize, learn and use effectively with animals. This, to my mind, opens up a whole new way of understanding animals. Dogs, particularly, can be a boon in this area, giving us plenty of opportunities to learn about and discover these signals. Unearthing more of these inherent communication abilities is going to be exciting, to say the least!

CHAPTER 4

THE CHEERWAL

Opt to Adopt

We always wanted Nishi to have canine company at home, but after her accident, she had developed a lot of fears, as expected, and had a lot to work through. She was getting into more and more fights with dogs she interacted with. We did not understand why this was happening to her, but we definitely did see that she was struggling with dealing with other dogs. I did not really want to push her into a difficult situation. I knew I had to wait for the right time and the right opportunity to know what was going to be best for her.

Meanwhile, I had started an online group, Bombat Dawgz, which had grown significantly and started revealing some very disturbing facts about the fate of dogs. Each day, more dogs are being created to keep up with the increasing demand of 'pets', and yet, people also seem to be abandoning dogs at an alarming rate. Shelters are bursting at the seams trying to keep these dogs safe until such time that they can find another home. Then, there are dogs that are picked up from the streets either because a litter is orphaned or a dog is injured and unlikely to make it on his/her own on the streets. These, too, end up in shelters. The most disturbing of all is the reluctance of Indians to adopt our indigenous dogs. I was increasingly finding it hard to claim to love dogs and yet willingly turn a blind eye to the fate of all these dogs. I questioned if I could genuinely call myself a dog lover if I am not moved by the lives of these dogs and have no will to make a difference to the life of at least one dog.

We bought Nishi believing that buying from a good breeder would ensure good health. One of Nishi's parents was a direct import and the other was some kind of a champion. Their health records looked squeaky clean. Still, she was plagued with genetic issues in her leg. As I learnt more about it, I learnt that almost all breeding experiments have resulted in a tremendous number of genetic issues in all species. In her book *Lost in Translation*, Temple Grandin discusses the odd case of roosters that were 'raping' other poultry and attributed it to breeding issues. She talks about how selective breeding focuses on some desired traits and that narrow focus of breeding programmes almost always has unintended consequences in the form of other traits changing. This is common across all species that humans try to breed. Dogs, in particular, are plagued with so many genetic issues that they are considered 'a boon' to the medical testing industry. John Bradshaw, in his book *Dog Sense*, explains, 'Rigid breed standards encourage breeders to eliminate all traits that don't fit the "perfect" type ... [This] has led to the appearance of an extensive range of inherited defects that compromise the welfare of large numbers of dogs in many, many breeds.' Dr Marc Bekoff in his book *Canine Confidential* argues that while good breeding practices are meant to focus on increasing genetic diversity, 'People still breed dogs who they know will have short and likely miserable lives because of inbreeding and selecting for traits that make it difficult for them to breathe or to walk. These people are essentially breeding for 'beauty over healthy', at the cost of empathy.'

To make matters worse, dog breeding has a very dark side in the form of puppy mills, and our country is plagued with them. Dogs are bred in the most inhuman of conditions. Dogs and puppies are often kept in tiny crates, not given enough room to move, made to live on top of their own excrement, sometimes their coat matted in all the filth they lie in all day. The female dogs are repeatedly bred, till they cannot breed any more and are unceremoniously discarded on roadsides. The puppies have the worst possible start to a life. The highly unhygienic conditions they are kept in can result in them contracting deadly diseases. The complete lack of mental stimulation, movement, parental care and social contact can have permanent impact on their brains, laying the foundation for a very difficult life.

If you have not already made the mistake of buying a dog, then you are in a place to make a difference. Take a moment to research puppy mills and see if you really think that the living being that you want to bring home as your friend for life needs to go through that kind of a start to a life just so they can make it into yours. Today, several parts of India are finally cracking down on this business of breeding and there are new laws springing up. So if you decide to buy a puppy, you may even be engaging in an illegal activity.

We do have an alternative in India—the dogs we informally call 'Indies'. These are a range of mixed-breed dogs, with a component of an Indian landrace called the INDog. These seem to be extremely hardy dogs that, given the right environment, can often live up to twenty years with very minimal medical intervention, if any. In my conversation with INDog expert Rajashree Khalap, she explains the superiority of natural selection over human-designed breeding programmes. Indies, unlike INDogs, are not aboriginal dogs. They are mixes of several breeds. They are, however, not a product of deliberate breeding and, to some extent, are shaped by natural selection. This is perhaps why they seem to be so healthy and live such long lives. Indies also do very well when it comes to dealing with the milieu of India, including our weather and space availability. They are also incredibly smart animals, often outdoing their pedigreed counterparts in most tasks that they are given a chance to do. Unfortunately, they have been dismissed for far too long, and their true potential remains undiscovered. What is most appealing about Indies to me is that because they are a mix of such a wide variety of breeds, pretty much any personality that we may be in search of is reflected in these dogs and one can be guaranteed to find a friend and companion in them.

Having gained this newer perspective, we were not going to buy a puppy from a breeder. Adopting a local dog just made sense ethically and practically. What was left to do was to figure out how.

Introduction to Fostering

One lazy weekend morning in 2012, as I stood on my balcony and sipped my coffee, I saw what looked like a lost Labrador. We decided to help reunite this dog with her guardian. We asked the people around to see if we could get some clues, but no leads came up. We needed to find a place to keep her until we could find her guardian. We could not take her home because Nishi was still not doing well with dogs.

I started browsing through the several requests for fostering dogs on Bombat Dawgz, hoping to find someone who had the room to foster this dog. I happened upon the picture of a ridiculously cute local puppy, put up by a local shelter. Something drew me to this photo. I started reading the details. There it was, the comment that found us our solution: 'I cannot foster puppies, but I can foster older dogs.' For some reason, I felt this was our answer. While I was not sure Nishi could handle a grown dog, I felt she might not be too terrified of a pup. So, I contacted the man who had posted the comment and told him that I had an adult dog that needed fostering, and in turn, I could try taking in the pup. In no time, the puppy arrived at our home. Her name was Rackles.

Rackles

We were now home with a beaut of a puppy. No dog I had seen ever looked so beautiful. Rackles was a firebrand. She was afraid of nothing. She walked into our house as if she owned the place. She took one look at Nishi and dismissed her. Then she looked around, found things to chew on and settled down with them. I have never seen a more confident entry into my house.

Nishi looked utterly baffled by this new creature in her home. She did not seem anxious, just curious and amused. And she was incredibly gentle too. The first time Nishi approached, Rackles snapped at her. Nishi retreated immediately. She did not approach Rackles any more, or at least that is what it seemed. Over the next few days, we observed the gap between the two reducing. I am not sure if Rackles was the one initiating closeness or Nishi.

Once they became friends, what followed were days of unadulterated play and joy. The big black dog of 40 kg and a wee caramel-coloured puppy—wrestling, tugging and chasing each other. However, the first few days were stressful for both. We saw Rackles have diarrhoea and Nishi pee on the carpet in the room. These are typical signs of stress. This knowledge will often help us understand a dog's behaviour better. It would have been easy to misinterpret Nishi's peeing as territory-marking to show dominance, which might have made us overlook the fact that the event was stressful for both dogs and that we had to find ways for them to cope with stress.

With Nishi's care and mentorship, Rackles was finally ready for adoption. I learnt about an adoption camp that was happening nearby, and I took my Rackles along. Most other puppies were scared and stuck to a corner. Rackles ran about the place like she owned it. She was the first puppy to get adopted. I was thrilled and heartbroken at the same time. Fostering is hard. Just when you get attached, the puppy is ready to go away. I was a weeping mess. After a tearful goodbye, I finally let her go to her new home. But Rackles was returned because the people who adopted her felt she was more than a handful. I am not sure they knew what to expect; they had likely not done their homework and suddenly realized they were in over their heads. So they made a feeble excuse about how they felt she was not happy to move into their house. They had acted irresponsibly. But Rackles got re-adopted as Mishka into the house of a lovely couple. Today, Mishka continues to shine like the brilliant star that she was born to be.

Foxy

At that adoption camp, I had seen a gorgeous copper-brindle dog with massive ears, like a bunny rabbit. Her name was Foxy, and I can vouch for the fact that she did live up to that name with her foxy looks and attitude. She was a stunner. She made her way into my heart quickly, as I saw her interact with her surroundings. She was bold, fearless and playful. I started wondering if she was right for us, but I was not confident enough to take the call just yet.

After Rackles left us, we fostered a few more pups and dogs. Nishi was doing really well. In fact, she was helping all these scared puppies and dogs come out of their shell and gain confidence. They would walk in as scared puppies, Nishi would shower them with patience and gentleness. They would quickly transform into happy and confident puppies! We now knew that the time was coming for us to take a call on adoption. Nishi seemed ready. Suddenly, our landlord asked us to vacate. Relocating stresses me out a lot, and I knew it stresses dogs out too, so we decided to hold off adoptions until after the relocation.

A few days after the move, Uttam and I started talking about the possibility of an adoption. We took into account all our perspectives, including Nishi's. Fostering showed us that Nishi could shed the crazy clown avatar and be a mature dog when she needed to be. She was responsible, understanding and, above all, patient. In fact, we learnt a lot about how to deal with new, scared puppies by observing her. She never pushed a puppy past its limits. She always respected boundaries but kept constant vigil on the pups. She won over each of them—slowly but surely. So we were all ready.

In all this time, I had not forgotten about Foxy. I went back and enquired about her and was devastated to find that Foxy was no more. Years later, I learnt that the facility that Foxy had ended up in was a bit of a horror house. The dogs were kept in tiny crates full of pee and poop, underfed, their water bowls unchanged. The dogs were rarely brought out.

Tigress

A few days later, I got a message from a lady called Debbie, who ran a shelter called Precious Paws Foundation. She told me that she had managed to rescue two dogs from the horror house Foxy had died in, and one of the dogs she had rescued was Foxy's sister, Tigress, who was now in her shelter. I knew what I wanted to do. We had to take Nishi to see Tigress. We wanted to meet Tigress too. If Foxy had been so full of oomph, I could not imagine what a dog called Tigress might be like! Nishi loved such sprightly pups, and I was brimming with excitement to see Tigress.

We went to the shelter and started looking around. Who could be our Tigress? The caretakers asked us what we were looking for and we eagerly said, 'Tigress.' They exchanged confused glances and pointed to the far end of the compound. There was Tigress, far away from all the pups, sitting hunched over, frozen, growling slightly and shaking in fear. She was older than I had expected, but small for her age. Nishi did not bother going anywhere close to her.

She was truly the underdog. It turns out that she had been at the adoption camp where I saw Foxy, but I did not recollect her at all. My friend, a photographer who had photographed that entire event, including Tigress, did not remember her. Another friend, who had groomed her too, admitted she could not recollect her. She was not friendly. She was scared and very understated.

We managed to coax Tigress to walk out to a large piece of land right outside the shelter. She did not seem to be the pup we wanted. I was looking for a dog that was happy and confident. We were not sure if we wanted to adopt this pup. However, the girls seemed to be effectively communicating with each other. Nishi had established her non-confrontational intent, and Tigress had expressed her need for extra space. Nishi was demonstrating that she had no intent to violate that space. It was touching to watch. An idea struck me. 'Uttam, why don't we foster? That's the least we can do in memory of Foxy. Let Nishi work her magic on her and get her out of her shell. We can then put her up for adoption.' Uttam saw the sentiment behind that decision and respected it. So, Tigress came home.

Once home, she dug a hole in the garden and settled down. She did not emerge for two days. On the third, when she did, it was only to growl at the very sight of Nishi. She nibbled a little on the food we had laid out and then retreated into the hole. I broke down looking at this. I told Uttam that I did not think fostering her was going to work. What I did not notice at all was that Nishi had been working her magic, and Tigress had been working hard to conquer her own fears. Gradually, she started to explore. In a few days, Tigress was inside the house!

Tigger

Despite moving in, space continued to be a big issue with Tigress. She wanted Nishi as far away from her as possible. If Nishi got anywhere close to her invisible perimeter, she growled. Nishi sat at the edge of the perimeter, never violating it and waiting for Tigress to see that she posed no threat. She sat facing away. Most times, it simply looked like she was ignoring Tigress. She was not. Dogs are subtle.

During meal times, Tigress would get very agitated about her food. At no point did we let Nishi close to Tigress's food. Not that we had to ask Nishi to do that. With all our foster experience, Nishi had already learnt that if a foster pup said 'stay away', she would respect that. As Nishi stayed away from the food, Tigress guarded it less and less. Today, I don't see any reason not to fast-track this process, by separating the dogs altogether, so that the new dog does not feel the need to protect their food and quickly gains reassurance that they are safe, that there is no need to watch their back when they eat—that they are home!

Dogs guard resources valuable to them, especially when they feel insecure about it. They guard food, space, objects and people. Tigress guarded them all. I am so glad we had Nishi because I don't think we knew the first thing about handling this situation. Nishi did. When I eventually met Turid and discussed it with her, I understood what was causing resource-guarding in Tigress and how Nishi had addressed it. However, even without understanding these things, we did do something right. We trusted Nishi. I don't know if we lucked out, but Nishi proved herself more than worthy of our trust by helping rid Tigress of whatever demons haunted her. Whatever I learnt from Turid and Nishi on the matter of helping a new dog cope is captured in the next essay.

Slowly, little Tigress started to emerge from her shell, and we glimpsed her true nature. She was a shy and mysterious girl. Affectionate and impish. We were falling in love with what we were seeing, and Nishi's bond with Tigress was getting quite strong. She was not the puppy I had imagined I wanted, but she was the puppy who made me fall in love with her. Nishi, Uttam and I agreed to adopt her. We let her into our family and our hearts. Tigress became Tigger or Tiggy—the shy, loving imp!

NEW DOG GUIDE

When getting a new dog, be it a puppy or an adult dog, one thing that we must acknowledge is that the move is stressful for the animal. Moving any animal from a known territory to an unknown one puts them on edge. In Nature, such a move is highly unnatural because it exposes the animal to unknown dangers, and animals usually refrain from drastic shifts in location.

When animals do need to migrate, a lot of caution and thought is put into it. Wolves are known only to move if their prey moves or prey density drops. Street dogs don't move very far from their territories either. Often, their explorations are limited to neighbouring territories, if at all. People who regularly feed street dogs will tell you that if a street dog has moved territories, then the dog is perhaps in a lot of trouble. The Indian Constitution too recognizes this, and it is in fact illegal to move a free-ranging street dog from one area to another.

In the case of our pet dogs, when they are moved to our homes, no part of the shift is in any way under their control. The dogs have very little understanding of what is being asked of them and nothing about it is natural. Moreover, they are being moved into a human being's home, which means that they are in close proximity to a whole set of other 'animals', who may or may not be hostile. For puppies, it may be the first time they have even stepped into an environment like our homes. Older dogs may be carrying baggage, which means that they may not interpret the move as good news. One way or another, we should expect a lot of confusion, stress and anxiety in our dogs and prepare adequately for it.

My earlier essay goes into a fair bit of detail on the physiological impact of stress and anxiety. So, right after a move, you should expect one or more of these in one or more of the dogs in the household.

- Diarrhoea or constipation
- Excessive peeing
- Lack of appetite or being insecure around food. While lack of appetite is a direct result of stress hormones, food grabbing can be a result of food insecurity.
- Excessive thirst
- An array of coping behaviours such as destruction, chewing, barking, howling and whimpering
- Sudden onset of a host of ailments including allergies, infections, dandruff and excessive shedding
- All sorts of 'odd behaviour', including being withdrawn, hyperactivity, aggression, fear, anxiety and depression

Given how varied the impact of stress is on the body and the many ways in which it can manifest, there is not really much people can do other than help the dog settle down as quickly as possible. The more we focus on their initial behaviour and try and do something about it, the more we are going to stress the dog out and possibly worsen the problem. The best thing that we can do for a dog at this point is give the dog a lot of space and time, and allow them to gradually learn to cope with their individual fears and anxieties by exploring the environment around them.

This is not the right time to do things like inviting friends over, training the dog, taking the dog on vacations, big moves or boarding. All of this will have to wait a little, until the dogs are settled in, know that they are safe and start perceiving the place as their home. For a dog like Nishi, this process took less than a few hours; for Tiggy, it took weeks; for some dogs, it can even take months. If you decided to be generous enough to give the gift of a home to a dog who might take months to settle down, then the most powerful thing you can do for your pet is give them space.

Giving space does not mean providing them a big house. It means not pushing the dog into doing things they may not be ready to do. Dogs, at their own pace, need to figure out that you are not a threat and that other things in the house are also not a threat. We cannot really do anything to expedite it. Sometimes in our eagerness, we can end up overwhelming the dog and slowing down the process. A general useful rule in dealing with dogs like this is to go slow. If you think you are going rather slow, go slower still. This is key.

You can start by offering the dog several choices, which will not only help you understand what brings them joy and happiness but also reinforce in the dog's mind that they are in a place where they are allowed to choose and be in control of their life, which in turn helps combat fear. There are studies that show us that having choice or even a semblance of choice and control over oneself goes a long way in reducing stress. It can also expedite a dog's bonding with their human. We could consider providing choices in things such as beds, foods, food bowls or walking equipment. Puppies can be given small, non-scary objects to explore, to build their confidence. Cosy corners are also important so a dog can retreat to a safe space; once they do, it is critical to not confine them or disturb them, so as to reassure them that there is a safe space that they can use when they feel overwhelmed and that they have control over when they walk in and out of it. During mealtime, it is best to leave dogs alone. Provide them with water close enough to their 'safe space' so that they do not feel like they have to 'overly expose themselves' in order to drink sufficient water.

When adopting older dogs or puppies that come from less-than-healthy environments, it is important to understand that some dogs can be so traumatized that they can emotionally shut down. It is easy to mistake this for obedience or calmness. Such dogs, when provided with the comfort of their own home, might start to feel better in a few days and venture out of their shell. This might, at first, look like sudden aggression, anger or hyperactivity. This is not to be mistaken for deterioration. In fact, some dogs may become naughty too, and that's a very good sign. However, if the emerging trait of the dogs is either fearful or aggressive, it might have to be dealt with. Either way, you can be sure that the dogs are now comfortable enough to start to express their emotions, which may actually be a step in the right direction.

As dogs show a willingness to explore, it is ideal to start providing them with just a little bit more to expand their mind. Do not overexpose puppies to big dogs without vetting the older dog first. Limit the number of dogs a puppy meets together at a time. Do not overwhelm puppies with long or busy active days. Take it easy in the beginning, because there is a lifetime of friendship that you are trying to get them to forge. Do not push the dog too far too soon, before the two of you have really got the opportunity to know each other and fall in love with each other. No matter how much due diligence we do, it is only after the dog moves into our house that we really get to know them, which is best done slowly and deliberately, at a pace that is comfortable for both.

Chemistry

As Tiggy came out of her shell, she built a bond with my sister's dog, Bella. The dynamics of their bond seemed strange to me at first. They played like best friends. During play dates, they ignored all other dogs and played just with each other, but they also got into fights. And how! I mentioned this to Turid and I asked, 'They are like sisters. I don't understand why they fight so much.' Turid replied, 'Have you noticed how badly siblings fight?' The light bulb in my head lit up. Of course! How could I have missed that? Tiggy and Bella were very close, age-wise, and were like sisters. Sisters fight like cats and dogs, if I may use that metaphor. Shringar and I had some fights that are perhaps in the school's wall of fame/shame. Shringar and I loved each other and yet fought viciously. We still maintain that status quo in our relationship—equal measure of love and fights. It's just inevitable. No wonder Tiggy and Bella fought so badly.

I know many clients who wish to have a second dog in the household to give company to their first dog. Many, though, don't seem to realize that they need to put thought into the chemistry between the dogs. Just like humans, dogs have opinions on other dogs. They take a shine to some easily, while they might develop an intense dislike for a few others. We reserve our right to like or dislike someone, but seem to give little thought to preferences of similar nature in dogs.

Getting a second dog is a bit like an arranged marriage in India. The dogs are being 'introduced', and we can only guess if there's going to be chemistry. I don't know how this pans out in marriages, but I do know that for dogs, there are a few things we can do to increase the possibility of them getting along. A two-year gap between the dogs often helps. In this case, the older dog finds it easy to take on the role of a mentor. If they are closer in age, then they are more likely to have the dynamics of siblings, which means lots of fighting, especially during the juvenile period of twelve to twenty-four months. A very large age gap may not work either. A very old dog may struggle with having a puppy or adolescent at home, which in turn can send the older dog into depression or constant irritation. Dogs of opposite genders usually make things smoother. Of course, none of these are set in stone. Just like with humans, it is almost impossible to predict if two people will get along. When in doubt, see if the dogs can tell you what they might have in mind.

I am so glad that in our household, Nishi and Tiggy get along famously. If we had Bella at home, with the two fighting siblings, who knows how we would have managed.

Fear

Our journey with Tiggy was one of understanding fear: Nishi's fear of big dogs, Tiggy's fear of just about everything, and their heroic conquest of both. Of course, our dogs did most of the work on their own, but they did need us to understand what they were going through and give them space to work their way through it. Our biggest contribution was simply developing a good understanding of fear itself.

None of us is a stranger to fear. It is a fundamental emotion shared across almost all species. So it should not be very hard to reach out to our own fears to develop an understanding of this emotion. We all have fears—some rational, some seemingly irrational. Because the fears our dogs experience often seem unjustified and irrational to us, our own irrational fears perhaps are a good place to start. Phobias typically fall under this category.

Long ago, I intensely feared the water. Human bodies are naturally buoyant. So logically speaking, that fear is unjustified. A classic technique to help us supposedly get over the fear of water is 'flooding'. Anyone who has had this technique used on them will perhaps be recoiling already. My swimming coach tried it on me: he'd fling me into 15-feet-deep water. It did not help. Instead, I became more and more afraid. My aunt would bring me to the pool. She would get me changed into my swimsuit. The second she got me in it, I would wait for the opportunity to bolt! My aunt used to chase me from one side, and my swim coach from the other. He'd catch me, and before I could wriggle out of his hands, he'd fling me into the pool. I choked and sputtered. I'd get out of the pool and vomit. In fact, just the idea of the pool made me nauseated. When my parents tuned in to swimming contests on TV, I'd get up and walk away. That's irrational fear! It has a way of making you feel terrible before your brain argues with you that it's unjustified. Watching swimming was not going to make me drown, but when fear takes over, thinking is altered. That's how all brains work.

While current neuroscience experts are changing our understanding of the way the brain functions and the way the tests on flooding were conducted, several professionals are questioning the ethics of this technique. I knew, from my own experience, that over-exposure to Nishi or Tiggy's fear triggers was not the way to get them to learn to cope with them. Instead, I tried to see if I could build positive associations with fear triggers, by offering them food rewards. That got me nowhere either. I could not understand where I was going wrong. The answer became evident one evening when Uttam and I were relaxing, enjoying some wine and good food. All was well, until I noticed a lizard on the far wall. I have an intense irrational fear of reptiles with legs. I tensed up and pleaded with Uttam to chase the lizard out. He was in no mood to run after a lizard and motioned towards the wine and food. 'Here, have some more of this amazing wine and forget about that lizard for now. It's nowhere close to you,' he said. I tried. I could not. I just could not get my attention away from it, until he eventually gave in, grabbed a broom and coaxed it out. I took several minutes after that to settle down. If I was unable to enjoy wine and chocolate in the presence of my fear triggers, more wine and chocolate would not help me learn to cope with my fear. Well, maybe the wine, until it wears off!

Getting over Fear

I did eventually learn to cope with my fear of swimming, but it was not with the help of my parents, aunt or coach. Fortunately, my parents had got tired of seeing me so miserable and had given up trying to get me to learn how to swim. Years later, I saw a flyer for swimming lessons stuck on the school bulletin board. I took down details and asked my parents if I could go. They were shocked. The unpleasant memories of the last attempt resurfaced, and they agreed under the condition that they did not have to be involved in any way. That was it. Once I started, I soon learnt swimming, and today, I love water so much that I am an advanced diver and have even considered becoming a diving instructor!

Uttam, too, had a severe fear of water, due to his near-drowning experience as a child. He decided to cope with his fear by learning to dive. To this day, his idea boggles me. How is it that one decides to cope with fear of drowning by strapping lead weights to one's waist and sinking to the bottom of the ocean? The point that becomes very evident during this discussion is that coping with fear is a very personal journey, which each of us does in ways only we understand. It also requires that moment of 'All right! That will do. I need to deal with this!' A moment of self-determination to do what we perceive to be rather difficult, to push ourselves to do something our instincts tell us not to do. It is driven by choice and cannot be forced.

One morning, I was sitting on the balcony, sipping tea. Uttam called out to me, asking me to hurry up towards him to see something interesting he had found. I walked up to him briskly. He held on to my shoulders, did not let me turn back and said calmly, 'Don't scream, but there was a lizard near your leg, that's why I called you away. I will chase the lizard away.' I sighed and hugged him for his consideration. When we love someone, we protect them from their fears, no matter how irrational it seems to us. My decision to do something about my fear of lizards is mine alone, and if I chose not to do something about it, nobody can do anything about it. The only thing anyone can do for me is to be considerate and offer protection. I'd hate to have to live with someone who constantly pushes me to be in the presence of my fear triggers.

When I discuss this idea with students, they often ask me if this means that we need to make peace with the fact that the dog will live their entire life with a certain fear. The answer is both yes and no. No, because dogs are overcome by curiosity and are more likely than not to want to learn to cope with the fear if they have the freedom to do it in their way and at their pace. Yes, because it was only when I eventually made peace with Nishi's fear that I fully let go of my expectations of her, thus giving her the choice and control she needed. I decided that she had as much right to fear as I did, and just as I needed my loved ones to understand my fear, Nishi needed us to understand hers.

If you recall, Nishi had developed a fear of Mojo and wanted to have nothing to do with him. Not knowing how else to help her, I gave up. During our walks, we avoided the street he lived on. One day, as we were out on our walk with Nishi, we approached the street Mojo lived on. Nishi stopped and stared. It did not last long, and I did not think much of it. However, the next day, she stopped at the same spot and took a few steps towards Mojo's house. The next day, she went further down the road. Eventually, she was standing in front of Mojo's house. We showered her with praise. Today, I know that she did not need that. She was doing this for herself. Conquering fear is inherently rewarding. It's one of the best feelings in the world. When it was time for Tiggy to learn to cope with her fear, we let the dogs take the lead. Nishi gave Tiggy lots and lots of space. Tiggy did the rest of the work on her own, going from a dog curled up in a hole in the garden to the gorgeous love-bug she is today.

UNDERSTANDING FEAR

Fear is the most commonly misunderstood emotion in dogs. It doesn't always manifest as a dog 'shaking in fear'. It can manifest in subtle ways or may present itself as 'aggression'. It is, therefore, very important for anyone working with an 'aggressive dog' to have a very good understanding of fear.

Fear is an adaptive emotion that helps us deal with danger or threat. It can cause certain metabolic changes within the body, which in turn affects their behaviour. It results in a threat response, or what is classically called the 'flight or fight' response, but it is not always as simple as this binary. Turid talks of the four Fs—fight, flight, freeze and fidget. We've already seen the biology of this response as SNS Activation. Many academics, psychologists and scientists have made attempts at classifying emotions, using various approaches. Some differentiate fear and threat response. Some fears are known to be innate, while some are supposed to be learnt. Some fears are supposed to be so easy to develop that it takes only a single exposure to develop lifelong fears. The field of fear has been extensively studied because human life is rife it, and thankfully so. Fear is what prevents us from being reckless and keeps us safe and alive.

We develop several fears through association, either through experience or observation. Dogs too have learnt fears, but some of those associations are not always obvious to us. For example, when Nishi met with an accident and a car ran over her face, she understandably developed fear—but of *dogs*, not cars. This is associative learning of fear that we discussed in Chapter 3. In Nishi's case, her attention was entirely on Mojo, and sure enough, she developed an intense fear of him and, subsequently, of large dogs. In her book, Turid explains this with another example of a dog who was intently observing a walker when a ladder fell, making a loud noise and scaring the dog. At that point the dog developed a fear of the man she was watching and not of the ladder.

To us, these kinds of strange associations are perhaps akin to human phobias. Phobias are described as fears that are excessive or disproportionate to the trigger. Many of them seem very irrational, and we are aware of this. Yet, the fear feels real and there is no arguing with it. Animals are unaware of the seeming irrationality of their fears. So, for them this fear is even more 'real'.

Another interesting phenomenon by which animals can develop fear is one where it has been passed down generations. Consider the following study on rats conducted by Emory University, which showed that if one generation of rats were subjected to prolonged stress and unpleasantness, in order to induce the fear of something, the next generation is highly likely to be born with that fear, without having to learn it afresh. Epigenetics is the study of heritable changes in gene expression that do not involve changes to the underlying DNA, which seems to be what is at play in these experiments.

While fear is ubiquitous and serves a purpose, it can also be paralysing. It is dangerous when expressed as aggression, and heart-breaking when it inhibits a happy, carefree life in a dog. These are situations in which we need to help them cope with their fear. How? One way is through exposure therapy, meaning trying to expose the individual to fear triggers in a mild form until they stop being fearful. However, there is no evidence that this destroys fear. Studies in animals show that even in cases where the fear seems to have been extinguished, it can come back very quickly with a single exposure.

Newer studies suggest that exposure therapy does not extinguish fear but builds new learning over it, which helps the individual cope. This is perhaps what we attempt when we try to build newer, more pleasant associations with fear triggers. But this too has its pitfalls.

These techniques of affecting behaviour modification may actually be resulting in the suppression of distance-creating signals. So far, there is absolutely no evidence of them actually affecting internal change—neither in the feeling of fear nor in the triggering of a threat response in a dog. The dog may suppress the behaviours that bother us but may still be experiencing the fear. This could convince us that the fear is gone and we may start exposing the dog to more and more of their fear triggers, eventually causing the dog to shut down or snap, without any warning signs. A shutdown dog may further strengthen our belief that the problem is completely gone. This is rather unfortunate, since the dog now suffers internally while we no longer have to deal with 'problem' behaviours.

Sometimes, it's tempting to believe that a large enough incentive can expedite the process of 'fear conquering'. The easiest place to see how this works is on popular reality television shows, where people are given very hefty rewards to incentivize them to fight through their fear. Of course, all the participants have the choice to walk away. Ultimately, only a few choose to brave all the tasks. It does not take a behaviour expert to see that fearful contestants do not actually *get over* their fears; most manage to bottle them up for long enough to get through a task, without meaningful long-term change.

Newer studies in the field of neuroscience show that the brain functions predictively, in that emotions are not responses to triggers, but the anticipation of it. So it is not the sight of a fear trigger that causes fear or a threat response, but the anticipation of seeing it, which the brain interprets as fear. This would then mean that a dog that is afraid of other dogs has their threat response turned on when stepping out for a walk, before they even see another dog. Trying to build positive associations after the appearance of another dog may simply be too late.

Fear is a very delicate issue, and every individual's relationship with it is nuanced. We simply do not understand it well enough, and one tiny mistake may push an animal past a threshold or get the animal to shut down. While studies are still trying to figure out how one extinguishes fear and how one could convert it to an administrable technique to a non-voluntary (not necessarily unwilling) participant like a dog, there is plenty of self-help on coping with human fears. Interestingly, almost all methods of coping with fear seem to involve *wanting to do it*, the ability to walk away and the freedom to use our preferred pace, internal dialogue and coping strategies. The journey away from fear is unique to the individual, who must find their own motivations, pace and coping mechanism.

If we were to assume this to be true of all animals, then would we end up getting stuck on step one with our dogs? I have not dealt with my fear of reptiles because I don't *want* to do so badly enough. Would we be stuck in a situation where a dog does not want to cope with his fear of other dogs or people, and therefore, continues to behave defensively? The good news here is that dogs almost always want to learn to cope with their fear, of both people and dogs. Dogs are hyper-social animals, and their survival depends on not being afraid of humans, artefacts in the human world or other dogs. So, there is a strong will, powered by the need for survival, that makes them want to cope with their fear(s). Consider the example of streeties. Many of them have been through severe abuse at the hands of other dogs or people, yet eventually, most of them learn to conquer it and continue to work with the environment around them. In my professional experience, I have observed that most dogs do want to cope with their fear. When they are kept at a safe distance from their trigger, they seem to be keenly interested and willing to slowly push those boundaries of safety. This is powerful for us to note, because it means that we do not need pieces of chicken meat or any other tasty treats to make a dog *want* to cope with their fear. Instead, we have something more fundamentally motivating and perhaps even more effective for a dog. In my work, I have come to count on this.

Conquering fear seems to involve new learning, a learning that tells an animal, 'I can cope.' A threat response, often associated with fear, interferes with this type of learning. Fear triggers the 'fight or flight' response, which generates cortisol, in turn interfering with the assimilation of information and inhibiting rational learning. It is now clear that conquering fear is actually a fine balance between exposing oneself to the trigger and still staying within the rational learning range of the brain. Given how complex this nuanced balancing act could be, the freedom to take control of the approach and the pace to figure this out is crucial for the animal. When I picture situations in which I have seen streeties trying to conquer certain fears, exploring things that they have previously been afraid of, I can see intense concentration. I can also see how even the slightest interference from me can damage the process to a point where I can induce more fear. Enticing dogs to stay closer to their trigger using food can also become too intrusive and interfere with the pace they need.

Learning to cope with fear involves exploring. To put this simply, curiosity seems to be the antidote to fear. A fearful animal is unlikely to be curious or to explore. The converse can be considered true as well—the more curious an animal is, the more he will explore and discover on his own that he can deal with what he was previously fearful of. Thus, the more opportunities we give a dog to explore while still feeling safe, the more their curiosity is aroused, which gives them a better shot at conquering their fear. The key here is the ability to enable curiosity, while preserving choice. Thus, the dog can continue learning even in the face of fear.

There is a subtle difference between enticing a dog to face their fear triggers and letting them explore those triggers on their own. Let me demonstrate with an example. Nishi has a fear of buses, and since it doesn't interfere with her day-to-day life in any way, we did not actively try to fix this issue. However, we recently discovered a lovely new clearing for Nishi and Tiggy's morning walks, but a lot of school buses are parked there. I wanted to see if we could manage this. Nishi and Tiggy consider our car a safe space. So I drove into the clearing, pulled up the car as far away from the buses as possible and left the car door open, with a ramp on it, so the girls had the option to run into the car any time they wanted to. It was very interesting for me to observe that both my dogs chose to get out of the car, but stayed very close to the car, moving in concentric circles around the car. Suddenly, one bus driver decided to drive his bus out of the clearing, which obviously frightened Nishi a lot. She ran back towards the car door, and I made no attempt to hold her back. When she reached the door, she went near the ramp but did not actually get into the car. Instead, once she realized she had the option of getting in, something made her stop dead in her tracks. She stood behind the ramp and watched the bus. She watched for a while as the bus driver struggled to manoeuvre the bus out. Slowly, Nishi seemed to realize that the bus was not going to hurt her, and she emerged from behind the ramp to resume her walk. It seems that the last memory Nishi registered in her head of this bus was that she knows how to deal with it. The next morning, it seemed that a miracle had happened. She was sniffing one of the buses and trying to see what was under it!

Tiggy, the Elf

Back to Tiggy! I call Tiggy an elf. If you are a *Lord of the Rings* fan, think of Galadriel. That's Tiggy. She is shy. She is wary of humans. She is nimble and elegant. She is magical, with a mysterious side to her. I find Tiggy quite an enigma. Often, she is lost in her own little world, rather busy staring at things I cannot perceive. We often get comments like, 'She must have a bit of fox/jackal in her.' Julia, one of my teachers (more on her later), says that Tiggy's body language is like that of a meerkat. Many of our native dogs and native dog mixes are a bit feline in their behaviour. This is rather pronounced in Tiggy. Approaching her is a lot like approaching a skittish wild animal, but once she gets to know you, she is gentle, like a deer. She has eyes that can mesmerize you. With her dainty paws, she will gently nudge you to pet her.

It does not take too long for her to switch from this avatar to a very scary one if something spooks her. She is not vicious. She does not bite, though I am sure if she were pushed far enough, like all animals, she too is capable of biting. I will always remember and respect that about all animals. Tiggy's scary avatar is meant to do just that—scare you away. She fluffs up to twice her size. Her beady liquid eyes narrow down. Her dark lips outline her perfect pearly white canines, giving them that dramatic effect. The brindle stripes on her face contort to something horrific and scary, like war paint on the faces of warriors and soldiers.

However, there is also a healing side to Tiggy's nature, which is the most mysterious of all. We first noticed this when she started licking Nishi's blind eye. Nishi lost vision and the tear glands of one eye during the accident. That eye keeps drying out. She has to have eye drops put into it every few hours. Ever since we got Tiggy, that job has reduced because Tiggy licks that eye. At first, we were concerned, but the vet convinced us that this was the best thing for Nishi's eye, because in some cases, surgeries are done to redirect saliva to the eyes. He asked us to watch out for possible infections, but we saw none. Instead, Nishi's eyes started to improve.

Having grown up in a family full of doctors, I must admit that I am a bit quick to rush to medical professionals, but Tiggy has made me reconsider this when it comes to her health. There was a time when she had a big lump on her foot. She was given some medicine for it. The lump did not subside. The vet then felt that it was time to remove the lump surgically, but I ended up travelling out of the country around that time. We were going to wait until I returned and then have it removed. By the time I was back, though, there was no lump. Tiggy had licked it off! Since then, we've made it a point to not give in to my urge to rush to the vet, but to wait and watch for a few days. I am fascinated that in all these years she's been with us, we've not needed a single medical intervention for her.

While I've been intrigued with Tiggy's seeming healing ability, the doctor's daughter in me remained sceptical until Tiggy decided to try it out on me. I once dropped a heavy whiskey glass on my foot, forcing the nail to come off. The foot suffered for days, and it was all rather disgusting. Tiggy kept trying to take a shot at it, but obviously, my rational brain resisted. One day, I finally gave in and let Tiggy lick it, bracing myself for the infection to worsen. Lo and behold, by the end of that day, I was looking at a mostly healed foot! While I remain a sceptic, I must admit that I am very intrigued by this dog.

Tiggy's ability does not stop at being able to heal. She seems to also know when not to attempt intervention. A few months ago, Nishi fell sick with a life-threatening communicable infection. When Nishi is ill, Tiggy is usually next to her, licking her and grooming her—but not this time. This time, Tiggy was far away and did not want to have anything to do with Nishi. Could it be because Nishi was sick with a contagious disease? While I cannot entirely understand how this works, I do know that animals are intuitive. They often know what is good for them and what is not. I suppose, then, that it should not be surprising that animals can have some innate ability to help themselves heal. It is perhaps required for survival. What that ability is and the extent of it is perhaps something science has yet to unravel for us.

Tiggy also seems to have an uncanny ability to know what to eat and what not to eat. Recently, I discovered Tiggy's love for almonds. Each morning, as I get a handful of nuts for myself, I give her an almond or two, and her eyes light up. A friend who visited us decided to gift Tiggy a bag of almonds, knowing her love for them. I offered Tiggy one of those almonds and she spat it out. The next morning, she was pleading for the almonds I was eating and crunched on them happily. On a hunch, I pulled out the almonds my friend gifted and offered Tiggy one of those, and she spat it out again. I then held one of the almonds from my morning stash in one hand and one from my friend in the other hand and offered both. Tiggy examined them closely and picked the one from my morning stash. I tried the experiment a few more times—same result. She knew what she was picking. It turns out that what I had at home were organic almonds, while what my friend had gifted were not. I repeated with a fresh pack of almonds and got the same result. It does make me wonder about the food we eat, the chemicals in them, the intuition of animals and what it could tell us about our own food habits. As I said, I do not exactly understand what is at play here, but I am intrigued enough to pay closer attention to Tiggy's actions, and those of animals in general.

Tiggy, the Genius

Tiggy is a bit of a genius. We often give our dogs puzzles involving food. They could be treats hidden below something, inside a box they must open or inside a bottle with a hole that they have to roll.

At first, Tiggy solved each puzzle elegantly. She lifted any container the treat was under. She gently opened boxes the treats were in. She rolled the bottle little by little, getting the treats out. Nishi, on the other hand, uses brute force. She smashes bottles. She jumps on containers until they break. Nishi is all about raw power. When she solves puzzles with strength, the deadly blow of her paws scatters the treats all over the room. Soon, we noticed that Tiggy had started to ignore her puzzle and would stand lurking around Nishi. While Tiggy's earlier solutions were smart, she had figured out how to be smarter still—and more elegant. She would simply wait for Nishi to solve it, and when all the treats tumbled out, she'd get some without Nishi even noticing. She would even offer her puzzle up to Nishi and wait for Nishi to smash it open. How very elegant and efficient!

Can animals understand mathematics? Obviously not in the way we understand it. However, I must concede that at least some of them have an ability that we do not fully comprehend. Tiggy seems to certainly demonstrate an uncanny superior ability to 'calculate odds'. She is a bit of a bully, so if she feels like she can bully a dog, she is very likely to do so, unlike Nishi. It is fascinating to watch how Tiggy determines if she can successfully bully a dog. Obviously, if she sees ill, old or small dogs, then she knows she can bully them. If, however, she sees such dogs in the company of a few other healthy dogs, then she will try to befriend them instead. Then there are times when Nishi is with her, and she feels 'her team' is stronger than the other dogs', in which case, she goes back into bully mode. Here too, if the opponent's group is large enough to seem stronger, she is back into friendly mode. Finally, if we are right behind her, then 'her team' is clearly the strongest, and she is ready to take on the whole group! Essentially, she calculates the odds of her winning and even re-calibrates rapidly if the situation changes. We have finally come to understand how Tiggy's mind seems to work and take the necessary precautions when she is meeting other dogs. We do not let her approach lone dogs that are unwell or old. If we do let her meet dogs, during their first encounters, we hold back Nishi and let Tiggy do it on her own. We try to stay out of it all as much as possible. We are quick to intervene if we see the situation changing, which is evident in changes in Tiggy's body language. While this does mean that we have to be as quick as she is, it also gives us yet another reason to be completely in awe of this fascinating creature.

Tiggy Becomes Cheerwal

The latest chapter of Tiggy's self-discovery seems to have led to a new identity altogether and is rather recent. One fine Sunday morning, Uttam and I were talking about a story where a dog seemed very unhappy with her name. It got us wondering if our dogs liked their names, and we both felt that Tiggy had never seemed very enthusiastic about her name. I had fallen into the habit of calling her all kinds of other names, and both Uttam and I noticed that there was one particular string of sounds that Tiggy responded best to—Cheerwal. To test if our observation had merit, I decided to call her by both names. I was shocked to see that she had a very clear opinion. She liked Cheerwal much better.

The next day, we told one of our friends that Tiggy had asked for her name to be changed. 'Cheerwal?' he asked. I was surprised that of all the names I call her, he too had noticed that she preferred this one. A few days later, a few of my students came over and decided to test my claim. They were in for a surprise. She just lit up when they called her Cheerwal. And so Tiggy became Cheerwal, or Cheeru.

Interestingly, the name change seems to have come at a time when her confidence was growing in leaps and bounds. The confidence extends to the realization that she is entitled to opinions and that we respect them. She also seems very thrilled with her new name and struts around the home with an air of self-importance. She sure has come a long way from the dog sitting at the far end of the shelter, growling at anyone who approached her. Shy, wary of people, magical, mysterious and scary—that's why Cheerwal is an elf like Galadriel. There is a lot I am still discovering about her and that she is discovering about herself. This new avatar of hers is pure joy, and I could not be more in awe of my mysterious Cheeru.

CHAPTER 5

UNLEARNING

Bad Wimpfen

I sat at a cafe at Frankfurt airport, waiting for a flight from Oslo to land. I was terribly excited and nervous. I had seen her picture on her book's cover, and I hoped that she did not look very different from it. I had waited a long time for this and could hardly believe it was finally happening.

Work with Nishi and Cheeru had led me to a Norwegian dog expert called Turid Rugaas. Turid changed my entire perspective on dogs. I had extensively communicated with her over email, and read all her books and articles, but I knew I needed to visit her because I could tell that there was more to all of this. Turid's courses spanned fifteen months, one weekend each month. Travelling to Oslo fifteen times or spending fifteen months in Oslo was not an option, so I continued to explore other ways of engaging with her. The perfect opportunity presented itself in 2013. I was then working as a VP at a Silicon Valley-based start-up but was on a sabbatical. One day, I received a rare and gracious offer from Turid to come stay with her and her students for a month. At the time, I was not sure I wanted to pursue a career with dogs, but I had started to reconsider corporate life. I was also starting to influence a lot of pet parents through Bombat Dawgz, the online group I had created, which had grown rapidly. While the cost of spending a month in Oslo was going be substantial, I knew this was an opportunity I simply could not pass up. So off I went.

I was to rendezvous with Turid in Bad Wimpfen, a little town outside Frankfurt, Germany. She was teaching a class there, and the weekend I was to land was supposed to be the last module of their fifteen-month-long education. This module would involve revisions and assessment. Turid felt it was a good opportunity for me to observe and get a gist of what her classes were about. We were to then travel together to Oslo. I had no idea what to expect, but I had a feeling that my life was about to change. What I did not anticipate was how much.

Finally, the flight landed, and she walked out. Turid was unmistakable with distinctive silver hair, tied together in her signature pigtails. I was in a tizzy and kept repeating to myself, 'This is really happening!' I was willing myself to get up and walk towards her, but excitement had paralysed me. Then, suddenly, a woman darted out of nowhere, grabbed Turid and gave her a big hug. That snapped me out of my trance, and I walked towards the happy women with the big smile on my face. I manage to get my voice to say, 'Hello! You must be Turid. I am Sindhoor. Big fan.' I stared at her with a silly grin on my face. I had planned for this moment for months. I had thought about many smart things to say, but all I could muster was 'Big fan.'

The Unlearning Begins

The next morning, I went to class not knowing what to expect. The students were curious about me and eager to know what I was doing there. 'How is your English so good?' one of them asked me. I smiled and wondered if a history lesson was due. They were also excited to educate me about their way of life and share with me what they had been learning for the last year and a half. They were warm and welcoming. I knew I was in the presence of like-minded people and felt eager to learn.

My first lesson came from a gentle and shy little Whippet. During the break, I went to meet this little Whippet. I sat down next to her, as I was used to doing with dogs back home, and started talking to her in an excited tone. The Whippet immediately turned her face away, yawned and quickly licked her lips. I was a stranger to her. She was shy and wanted to take a bit more time to see how she felt about me. I would imagine, having learnt about calming signals, I'd see this and recognize it for what it was. Turns out that most of us are blind to subtle communication. Some of the students had to point out to me that the dog was giving me calming signals to tell me that she was uncomfortable with the way I wanted to interact with her. I did not like what I was being told and got up and walked away, muttering to myself, 'Oh, loosen up, will you? I was only sitting next to the dog.' That was just the beginning. Over the course of that weekend, I had to unlearn a lot more, learn a lot and accept how little I actually knew.

The Barn

Once we all got our coffee, I was told that we were going to head into a barn. Coming from a city in India, I'd never been in a barn. 'What's in the barn?' I asked the students. 'An enriched environment,' they responded. I looked forward to doing whatever one does in an enriched environment in a barn.

The barn was much bigger than I expected, but what was on the inside was far more unexpected. There were cans and bottles hanging from metal frames, old cycles, old tyres … all kinds of rubbish. In fact, it looked like a junkyard. Well, maybe not as bad, but it was really a collection of odds and ends. The dogs were brought into this environment, one at a time, and just given the freedom to explore all of it at their own pace. The dogs seemed to love it. I was told that it does wonders for their mental health and fosters healthy curiosity. When I returned home, I set up something similar, executed a bit differently to work in a small city apartment, and I called it the 'enrichment bucket'. Just a fancy term for a bucket full of rubbish that I put out for the dogs that come in for a consultation.

One of my students to whom I explained this concept giggled and said something like, 'I spend so much money on buying expensive toys for my dog, and yet, at the end of the day, all he wants to do is play with this stuff. I am sure he likes this better, and it is definitely cheaper on my pocket.'

ENRICHMENT FOR DOGS

The field of mental stimulation in humans has been extensively researched in the context of preventing or delaying Alzheimer's. The idea is that mental stimulation can increase the neuron reserve, and a larger reserve can offset the losses caused by Alzheimer's. In the context of our dogs, increasing neuron reserve is necessary not only for puppies learning about the world, but also for adult dogs learning to cope, and in senior dogs to prevent Canine Cognitive Disorder, a condition similar to Alzheimer's in humans.

Exercising the brain is about providing information through the senses that the brain finds novel or challenging. The brain processes it, learns from it and stores it, but the exposure must be gradual and must not overwhelm the individual, because fear has a negative impact on learning. Turid calls this 'vaccinating the dog to the world'. The idea is to provide exposure to new things and always remain within the dog's ability to cope. If dogs get overwhelmed at any point, they may shut down.

In a city like Bangalore, it's quite hard to find the right balance between challenge and overexposure. The countryside is ideal to provide an animal with just the right exposure. However, metropolitan cities can get too busy, to the point where dogs are not able to cope, resulting in over-stimulated dogs. In some other cases the pet parents themselves may find it difficult to cope with the challenges of taking their dog out. In such cases, the dogs may end up confined indoors or locked out in the yard all day long, so they have nothing to look forward to and nothing new to experience. Such dogs are under-stimulated. Finding the right balance in a busy city is indeed challenging, and this is where we need to get smart.

To make it easier for my clients to find the best way to mentally stimulate their dogs, I ask them to think of it as introducing novel inputs through the senses, both indoors and outdoors. For example, could there be a way to introduce new tastes? You could offer your dog two bowls of water—one with regular fresh water and the other with a drop of curry or tea to bring in some interesting flavours. Perhaps introduce new ingredients in their food: different vegetables, meat sources, herbs or oils. Some dogs are very visually oriented and seem to get a lot of mental stimulation through their visual experiences. One of my clients had an interesting walking routine. His dog was very skittish and could not handle the busy streets of Bangalore. Instead, they spent some time each evening sitting in silence under the shade of a tree, right next to a gap in the compound wall through which the dog would watch the road outside. Her human saw this as an opportunity to cut off from all gadgets and spend some time under the light of the setting sun in the cool evening weather, relaxing and unwinding after a long day. Sometimes, it might be a good idea to take dogs out for a car ride to a marketplace and let them observe from a distance—taking in the sights, smells and sounds of a market from the safety of a car. In our car, we have removed the backseats completely and created a place where my dogs can comfortably sit and look out through the huge rear window. It's very amusing to watch them, since they look like they're watching a picture on a big TV.

Of all the senses of a dog, the sense of smell is what needs the most attention. They have an incredibly powerful nose. The percentage of a dog's brain involved in processing olfactory input is around forty times greater than that in humans. While humans have 6 million olfactory receptor sites, dogs have up to 200 million. The number goes up even higher to 300 million in scent hounds such as Beagles. Anne Lill Kvam, in her book *The Canine Kingdom of Scent*, offers an interesting anecdote just to put this into perspective: 'As humans, we may be able to smell sugar in our coffee if several spoons were added. A normal dog, on the other hand, would be able to sniff out one spoon of sugar in two Olympic-sized swimming pools.' While we have a single olfactory organ (nose), dogs have two (nose and the vomeronasal organ in the upper palette). When we think about the magnitude of this ability, it makes us wonder if we are anywhere close to stimulating a dog enough on this front. Streeties, of course, have a lot to sniff. They live in a very interesting landscape. Unfortunately, our dogs don't have access to such a variety of smells. Whatever odours we may have in our houses we seem to systematically get rid of with cleaning agents and detergents every morning. While we do take our dogs out on walks, we don't always provide them with enough opportunities to sniff. We walk them rapidly on busy streets where they find it difficult to slow down and explore the environment calmly.

I loved the barn in Bad Wimpfen. But when I came back to India, I realized that this idea was not meant for us. Neither do we have large spaces like barns, nor do we really need them. Our roads are plenty enriching, as long as we figure out a way to moderate the stimulation and provide our dogs with an environment that does not overwhelm them.

Another alternative to the enriched environment in the barn is an 'enrichment bucket'. An enrichment bucket is a collection of interesting odds and ends found lying all around the house. There is really no limit on all the things I can put in there. My dogs love exploring boxes, bottles, old clothes, old gadgets ... you name it. I also try to look for things outside the house, such as branches, pods and feathers, and add them to the bucket. However, we must remember that dogs are neophiles and need something new each time. We could use a few little tricks to get them excited about our enrichment bucket. My first trick is to not leave the bucket around them all the time. I bring out the bucket only once a day for an hour, express a lot of excitement when bringing it out, put it all away once the activity is done. I recreate that same atmosphere of excitement the next time I bring it out. The second trick I use is to make sure to put something new in it every day, so they have something new to find each time. I work with objects that offer different smells, textures, tastes and sounds. Some might roll, while others might create a scratching sound when on the ground. They are all learning experiences for the dogs. My final trick is to cut up small pieces of tempting food and scatter it around the enrichment area. If I am dealing with multiple dogs, I set up multiple stations to give them some choice and space. Once I have set it up this way, which does not take me more than a minute, I let them handle things on their own and do not interfere in their process of exploring. I wait for them to entirely lose interest to pick up the objects and put them away.

The Internet is a great resource to find DIY puzzles to create for your dogs. Some of them are very innovative, while some can cause injuries in dogs or can get them very hyper. It is important for you to use your judgement and try to pick games where dogs have to think more, rather than senselessly try to chase after things. In the recommended reading list, I have included a fantastic book on scent games.

Out of all the tools in my tool belt, I find the most effective one to be explorations or sniffaris. Our usual walks were just not working. My dogs would get far too stressed or excited, which made them pull. This, in turn, made them more hyper, stressing me out and straining our relationship. It was becoming a chore that no one looked forward to. Instead, what we do now is go on sniffaris. The dogs are taken to their designated pee and poop area, where they are comfortable relieving themselves. This is decoupled from their exploration time. The sniffari is done in different, interesting places that offer a somewhat relaxed space for dogs to sniff. A parking lot late at night can be fun, where vehicles tend to have a lot of smells of different dogs that have peed on them throughout the day. Sometimes, we drive out to a quiet street early in the morning or find a site for sale that might have been cleared. It could be an abandoned ground or a construction site. Parking lots of bars tend to be empty during mornings. Once you start looking, you will see the options. Since dogs can gather so much information from just one little spot, they don't need much space, especially in a country like India.

When a dog actually smells another animal's poop, they are not doing something disgusting. They are simply gathering critical social information. A dog who smells another dog's poop or pee is able to determine things like the other dog's age, gender and health; whether the dog is on heat or not; what the dog might have eaten; when the dog might have passed by this spot; which direction the dog came from; which direction the dog went; and even who accompanied the dog. If a dog is gathering all that information from just one piece of poop, you can imagine what a dog gathers on a ten- to fifteen-minute intense sniffing exploration of a small piece of land. When a dog's brain is engaged so intensely, they cannot sustain it for too long. They become quite exhausted, and when they return home, they need to sleep for long hours.

Jaak Panksepp says that 'seeking' is one of the primary emotions that all mammals feel. Seeking triggers joy in the brain. This emotion is said to be brought about by things such as curiosity, anticipation, interest and problem-solving. Basically, it feels good to be interested in what is going on around us. This is what Dr Sapolsky calls 'being high on life'. This does not mean that one has to be hyper-aware—just curious and interested. Curiosity can be a good barometer for mental health and is also one of the many great assets of a dog. Therefore, curiosity must be nurtured and adequately stimulated to maintain a good level of mental and physical well-being in our dogs, and perhaps in most animals.

Observing Dogs

Back to the barn in Bad Wimpfen, as I looked at the 'enriched environment', I wondered what the dog was supposed to do. I asked one of the students, who said that nothing specific was expected of them. I asked her what we were supposed to do. 'Observe!' she said. 'Observe what?' I asked. 'The dog!' she said, sounding a little exasperated. So I stopped asking questions and decided to watch. The little Whippet from earlier was brought in and let loose. She ran in a frenzy for a few seconds, then slowed down and started sniffing. 'She is doing so much better. She has slowed down considerably,' Turid commented, and they all agreed. 'Why should she slow down?' I asked the student I had been bugging. 'Because otherwise, they will have no brains!' she exclaimed. That made no sense to me. It was the beginning of a lot of things that did not immediately make sense to me.

It has taken me a while to understand what I was being taught back then. Today, I know that the frenzied running has to do with increased adrenaline, and if we do nothing to address a dog being in that heightened state of arousal for too long, they would soon start exhibiting other related behavioural and physical problems. I do like watching a dog run. By the time I visited Norway, Cheerwal was in my life and she ran like lightning. It was pure joy to watch. However, Cheeru would not only run but also do frequent 'zoomies', which was a very frantic running around in aimless circles. While we see many animals run, we don't often see other animals display such frantic behaviour often. We don't see streeties do it. Why do we accept this as normal with our pet dogs? There really is nothing wrong with a dog running, and some amount of running is, in fact, good for the joints. But frequent zoomies are another matter and should make us examine the dog's life for sources of over-stimulation.

As I sat in my hotel room in Norway, ruminating over the ideas I had learnt during the day, I felt uneasy. I had been through hell and back with my dogs. I believed I had given them my all and that no one could love them as much as I did. I believed I would never do anything to hurt them. Admitting that I might be doing something that might possibly have hurt them in some way was not easy. One part of my brain refused to admit that I might have been wrong, while the other knew the inevitability of the admission. For the rest of the evening, I refused to think about what I knew I needed to think about and decided to take in the beauty of medieval buildings in the village of Bad Wimpfen instead.

Sit!

The next day, I decided I wanted to take it a little easier on myself. I avoided conversations with people and tried to hang out with just the dogs. Someone had a few treats around, and I decided to offer some to a dog. Out of habit, I held the treat high and asked the dog to sit. Immediately, a few students came up to me and sternly informed me that they don't ask their dog to sit. 'Oh,' I said, but dared not ask why. I was afraid of more information that would make me uneasy, but the students told me anyway. It was newly acquired knowledge for them, which they were eager to share.

Later, when I got the opportunity, I decided to talk to Turid about it. I explained to her that I would only ask Nishi to sit when in an elevator or when greeting guests. I felt like I was not overdoing it and that I really needed to do that to manage a hyperactive dog like Nishi. Turid looked at me blankly and said, 'You said that your dog has a bad knee and has had surgeries on it. You ask that dog to sit?' I was stunned to silence. I held back my tears, asked a classmate to drop me back to my room, and I cried.

The accident was not the only trauma in Nishi's life. She suffered from a genetic condition called patellar subluxation, which causes severe pain in the knee. She had been through several surgeries and months of physiotherapy to be able to even land any weight on her leg. I did not need to be told that she struggled to sit and get up. It was evident by just looking at how laboured her actions were. But because Nishi would jump on guests and people in elevators, I had trained her to sit on command. I would insist that she sat whenever we were in an elevator or for the first few minutes when we had guests over. This meant that she had to sit on command, at least four to six times a day. There was no more escaping this internal dialogue I needed to have. I was asking my Nishi to do something painful four to six times a day, because I believed that it was the only way to do things.

Uttam and I had argued about this on several occasions in the past. I had diligently cut up several treats and put them in cookie jars near the door. I had instructed Uttam to carry several with him when he took Nishi in the elevator,

Streeties are often polite and relaxed in their interactions with humans. They forge friendships quickly, seeking contact and affection. Food is not their only priority.

Streeties can often be seen perched at a height. They demonstrate excellent judgement and find efficient ways to descend gracefully.

In India, for the most part, streeties co-exist peacefully with other free-ranging animals like pigs, goats, cows etc.

Streeties are seen sleeping on elevated surfaces, assuming different postures, often in the company of other streeties.

Many dogs like sleeping with their head elevated or dangling from the bed. This is often driven by neck pain, which is quite common in dogs with instability in the hips and knees.

A construction worker gets some tea, while her dog friend waits patiently. This is an example of the informal relationship several people have with dogs, which does not include 'ownership' but only mutually beneficial companionship.

Dogs are highly expressive animals and can emote very well with their face and eyes.

Nishi expressing joy.

Nishi expressing disappointment.

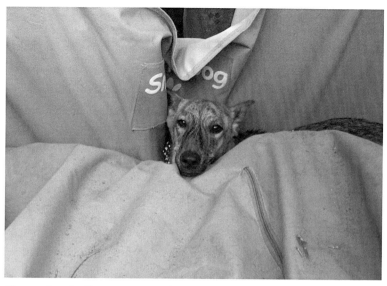

Cheeru when she first came to us and was nervous.

Cheeru today, using the power of her eyes to beg for food.

Dog TV: Looking out of the rear window of our car is visual sensory input and acts as mental stimulation.

Exploring things at home and in the garden can provide mental stimulation to dogs.

Car tyres carry a lot of exciting information for dogs, and a trip to the parking lot can be enriching for them.

Sniffaris can be conducted anywhere, as long as the dogs get plenty of time to sniff.

to command her to sit and to treat her appropriately. He was not so diligent about it. This led to arguments. I blamed him for being lazy. He argued that he just did not like the idea of having to ask Nishi to sit. I felt that after I had learnt from Turid, he would take me a bit more seriously and would participate in Nishi's training. Instead, I found myself calling him, sobbing and apologizing for having gotten it all so wrong. This was the first of many such weepy calls that month.

SIT!

The history of training 'sit' takes us back to Europe in the 1880s. There seems to be an early reference for 'sit' being used on circus dogs as early as the 1860s and hunting dogs in the 1870s. However, it was not until the 1920s that 'sit' really started to become popular, when competition obedience was introduced. From there, it spilled over to households through pet dog training. In India, it is still not very common; it is almost unheard of in rural India. In the western world, 'sit' is used quite ubiquitously in many situations—to ensure that dogs don't bolt out when opening doors, to prevent a dog from jumping when serving them their meals, before receiving treats, before putting on the leash when taking the dog out on a walk, when meeting visitors and guests etc. It is almost considered default 'good behaviour'. Most dog training tutorials begin by teaching 'sit'. I trained my Nishi to sit on cue because I felt like it gave me a better sense of control over the situation and that it calmed her down when she was being hyperactive.

The question, however, is if it actually works the way we want it to. It did not, for me. It was hard to make Nishi sit when there were no treats with me or if the magnitude of distraction was too high. Incidentally, this is when I needed the 'sit' command to be the most reliable. I was also seeing that even in situations where dogs hold the sit, they seem to bounce back with extra energy once they are given the release command. It was certainly true of Nishi around guests. Most of my clients complained of this too.

While there are not enough studies on this topic, I was able to find one interesting study by Miller et al. that suggests that making a dog sit may actually be counterproductive when it comes to their social interactions. In this study, dogs were asked to wait for a bit and then given a series of tasks to perform, whilst the researchers measured how focused they were during the tasks. Some of the dogs, however, were asked to hold a sit position while waiting. These dogs rapidly lost their focus and gave up on subsequent tasks more easily than the dogs who were not asked to sit while waiting. The dogs were then asked to be in the proximity of a caged reactive animal. The dogs who were asked to sit were two times, or 200 per cent, more likely to react aggressively.

What might be happening here? While the study suggests that it is a depletion of self-control, I look at it more from the perspective of preventing functional behaviour. Behaviours do not exist in isolation. They are meant to serve a function for the animal. For example, when my dogs see street dogs from a distance, they sniff the ground. Sniffing the ground may serve the purpose of communicating with other dogs or an attempt to calm themselves down. When the dogs start interacting, they start using calming signals like sitting, lying down, freezing, sniffing, turning away, walking in a curve and even walking away. While sitting is a calming signal as well, Nishi prefers not to sit in tense situations where she may need to move quickly. This may be due to her bad knees or perhaps it is just not the right signal for the context. She seems to prefer to freeze and turn her head, and I can see how effective it is when she is trying to forge new friendships. Nishi is often eager to make friends. Cheerwal is more cautious about making friends. So she sometimes stands with her hackles raised and her teeth bearing. This behaviour is meant to serve the function of letting other streeties know that she is not ready to meet them and would like them to walk away. Sitting is unlikely to be communicate the right message in this context and will not serve her purpose.

Basically, by asking dogs to sit in these situations, I had, in effect, confined them, reduced their movement and taken away their choices and their ability to use the necessary communication signals. Taking away choices increases stress response in animals. In addition, interfering with their communication could negatively impact social interactions and may lead to misunderstanding and perhaps even fights or learned helplessness.

Consider the situation where dogs are asked to sit to avoid the excited jumping when meeting people. Jumping up and down is part of a biological response to increased adrenaline, which makes an organism want to move. Think of children who are very excited about an impending activity and are consequently pacing, or running up and down. Imagine their parents yelling at them, 'Sit down!' It is easy to deduce what might happen next. Even if they manage to sit down, it is likely that they will start fidgeting, tapping their feet or talking nervously. By insisting that our dog sits, we are not only discounting their need to move but also taking away opportunities for other, more acceptable behaviours that can help them cope. Biologically, not being able to engage in coping behaviours can increase stress response.

Consider this experiment in which rats were administered a mild static and their stress levels were measured. Their cortisol levels increased as expected, but what is interesting is that in the subset of these rats who were given access to a bar of wood to gnaw on, cortisol levels dropped significantly. Gnawing on wood clearly serves the rat a purpose. Similarly, something as simple as picking up something in their mouth and running might help our dogs cope. Having them sit through things will take away their opportunity to find an alternative coping strategy.

Then there is the question of dogs with bone, joint and muscle issues. Many of my clients' dogs had joint stability that largely remained undiagnosed. These undiagnosed conditions often manifested as hyperactivity, since discomfort increases cortisol in the body. Owing to their hyperactivity, these were being made to sit a lot by their pet parents, in an attempt for them to regain control of the situation. However, sitting clearly made things worse for them.

By making 'sit' such an integral part of the everyday lives of dogs, could we risk taking away the option of not sitting if it becomes uncomfortable for dogs or the ability to engage in functional behaviours? We know that removing choices can trigger stress responses. Increased stress response alters an animal's ability to focus, and that perhaps explains Miller's study results on the tasks dogs had to do. Not engaging in coping behaviours can also cause frustration in dogs, which can trigger their rage system. The firing of the rage system in the brain can lead to aggression.

Turid asks her students to do a 'sit study', where we are required to observe the sitting preferences of a dog when they are not actually asked to sit. Some of the observations are quite interesting:

1. Some dogs sit a lot, while some don't sit at all. This could be based on individuals, but it could also be because of breed traits. Sighthounds, for example, did not want to sit at all, while Bulldogs seemed to want to sit for long periods of time.

2. Some dogs wanted to sit and watch what was happening around them, but many dogs did not stay seated for very long. Many transitioned to lying down very quickly.

3. Some dogs seemed to sit because they cannot breathe easily when lying down. Bulldogs, Pugs and other brachycephalic dogs fall into this category.

4. Many dogs do sit when interacting with humans and trying to ask them for things. Given that dogs use their eyes a lot to convince people to ask for things, it is easy to see that they perhaps find it easier to sit so they can continue to look up at us for long periods of time.

5. Dogs seem to have different kinds of postures they like to use when they sit. Some seem to stretch their legs out, while others lean to one side. The sitting posture of a dog is largely an indication of the muscles and joints they are trying to protect, which they intend to use to power the lying down or getting up motion.

6. Interestingly, regardless of personal preferences and musculoskeletal issues, if they are specifically commanded to sit or they were using the sit

position while interacting with humans, they were more likely to do a balanced square sit.

7. Arthritic dogs, dogs with hip dysplasia, dogs with patellar subluxation and other similar injuries are, in general, reluctant to sit and reluctant to get up once seated. Many tend to not use the appropriate limbs to power this action.

While sitting is a natural action, there is a need for appropriate usage—just like with humans. We need to account for personal preferences based on seating surfaces, health of the individual, physical abilities and limitations. We must take cognizance of the fact that repeated movements are just as likely to lead to RSI (Repetitive Stress Injuries) in dogs as they are in humans.

Nishi struggles to sit and needs a lot of help. Cheerwal is not in as much pain, but still seems to have a hip stability issue that remains undiagnosed. Asking either of them to sit is not really an option for me. So, I have been forced to get better at using body language for communicating in many situations, like when preventing them from bolting out of the house or jumping on me when I'm serving a meal. When I am unable to use signals and body language, I try to use clever management to avoid the situation altogether. I now have alternatives for everything. I no longer need 'sit' to manage any situation with my dogs.

Dogs seem to be inclined to sit when interacting with humans, which makes it very tempting to use it as much as possible. However, it comes at a cost for many dogs. Just two generations ago, my grandfather did not need it. Its use is not as ubiquitous as we think. It is definitely worth questioning this training tool and exploring other options where we do not need to use 'sit' to achieve what we want.

Fetch!

This trip was not exactly turning out the way I had imagined it would. My success with helping Nishi deal with her fear of Mojo and my subsequent experience with the rescues and fosters back home led me to believe that I knew a lot about dogs. I thought that visiting Turid would make me better by giving me more tools to add to my tool belt. But here I was, feeling more like I was being stripped of the tools I had, making me feel a bit despondent about my ability to deal with dogs.

While all of this was new for me, the German students had been learning and internalizing these ideas for more than a year now. They had perhaps forgotten how shocking these messages are for someone who hears it for the first time. They, enthusiastically and a bit tactlessly, delivered to me the next difficult message: fetch is bad. That meant I had lost another tool! I had read that fetch was a great way to burn the energy of a hyperactive dog and sit to be a wonderful alternative to unwanted behaviours. I had painstakingly gained this knowledge by reading several books, so I was not willing to let go of them just yet.

'What is wrong in playing fetch if it calms my dog down and makes her feel happy?' I asked Turid, rather defensively. 'It does not calm them down, it makes them hyper, and they do not feel happy, they are hysterical,' she explained. I was not convinced. 'Why do you believe it does not calm them down?' I demanded to know. One of the students spoke up and asked, 'Have you noticed the burst of energy after a workout in the morning?' That was indeed food for thought. I had been through phases in my life where I exercised extensively. I knew it to be true that when I worked out at night, I did not calm down, but struggled to fall asleep for at least an hour after. Exercise releases adrenaline and cortisol. Cortisol takes up to an hour to clear and is also known to interfere with sleep. When I ran marathons or practised dance for hours, before my Rangapravesha, those were the worst. My body would be exhausted and would want to sleep, but my mind struggled, and so, while I'd fall asleep for a bit, I would be up again very quickly.

The call I made home that evening was very different from the one I made the previous night. Uttam loved playing fetch with Nishi, and I knew it was going to be very difficult for me to talk him out of it. As I explained the ideas to him, I heard his scepticism on the phone. I knew this was going to be a long battle. However, years later, when I met Julia Robertson, a muscle therapist for dogs, she too spoke about the ill effects of fetch, but this time from a muscle perspective. She brought videos that showed us the kind of damage that a game of 'fetch' causes to the muscles, which eventually convinced all the non-believers in my family that we had to find alternative ways to engage with our dogs.

Letting go of fetch was not easy because of how happy Nishi looked when she played. Having said that, dogs don't need to play fetch to be happy. Dogs can find a lot of joy in good food, healthy social interactions, exploring interesting things and feeling a certain sense of control over their own life and destiny.

Geithus

The weekend in Bad Wimpfen had taken a toll on my confidence. The plan for the following week was for me to return to Oslo with Turid and to spend ten days with her at her place in Geithus. Not surprisingly, I was nervous. I pretended to sleep on the flight and made poor attempts at conversation on the drive from Oslo to Geithus. We eventually pulled up at the Hagan farm, a gorgeous, quaint property set by the fjords of Norway. As we prepared to get out of the car, the door opened, and we were greeted by Turid's daughter, her granddaughter, and her dog McKenzie. I watched them greet each other and stood by awkwardly, hoping that I would not get the greeting protocols all wrong. I was going to be staying in this house for the next ten days, with people who knew nothing about me and yet had opened their home to me. I knew nothing of them either. Suddenly, I started wondering what I had gotten us all into. I was beginning to panic, when suddenly, McKenzie bounded up to me. Once he came up to me, the uneasiness of the unfamiliarity around me vanished. I was in the presence of the familiar—of a dog. No smell in the world is more familiar and comforting to me than the smell of a dog. I dropped my guard, got on my knees and petted him.

Once McKenzie greeted me, the rest of the family followed suit and extended me a warm welcome. I was led inside what turned out to be a beautiful, cosy Norwegian home. I spent the rest of the evening with the family, getting to know them better and telling them a bit about my own dreams and reasons for being there. Eventually, I was led up the stairs to my room that overlooked the woods. It was late, and the window opened out to pitch darkness. I'd like to say that I sat by the window, lost in poignant thought. The truth is that I just crashed. I had had a weekend full of intense, thought-provoking discussions, and my brain had used up the last of its resources to keep up. It needed to recharge. I fell asleep and passed out like a log.

The next morning, I woke up rather disoriented. It took me a while to figure out where I was. Oh yes! I was at Turid's place. I was there to learn. I wondered what the day would be like. And how many more difficult lessons I would have to learn—not to play fetch with my dogs, not to hug my dogs, not to ask them to sit. I thought of the adage about ignorance being bliss. I sighed, shook off my anxiety and decided to face whatever the day had to offer.

Turid and Kenzie

Observing Turid and Kenzie was fascinating. Kenzie seems to be the most perfectly behaved dog on earth. Mind you, I am not saying that he was the most obedient dog on earth. He just seemed to know the appropriate behaviour in any given situation. Turid would sit on her porch while Kenzie explored the farm. It was adjacent to the woods, but he always stayed close and somehow seemed to know exactly when Turid wanted him to return home. He never bolted out of gates and knew the right time for him to walk out of it. When they went out on walks, she would put a leash on him—but a very long one, which seemed to be there only because the leash laws required it to be there. The leash was long enough to allow him to wander around her at a respectable distance. They seemed to generally move in the same direction and simultaneously decided when it was time to return. They were clearly a team!

One day, Turid, Kenzie and I were sitting outside, enjoying the fresh air from the woods, when suddenly, Turid and Kenzie got up and walked back into the house. I was a bit taken aback. I was not sure what had just happened. Were they going to come back? Was I supposed to follow? I waited there for a bit and then went into the house looking for Turid. 'What just happened? Why did you suddenly leave?' I asked her. 'Oh! Did you not see what Kenzie said?' she asked. Obviously, I had no clue. 'He indicated that there was something in the woods!' she explained. My jaw dropped! When we had arrived at Geithus, Turid's daughter had informed her that there had been sightings of bears and wolverines in these woods. After this, I decided to pay more attention to the more subtle interactions between Turid and Kenzie.

I eventually discovered that Turid and Kenzie communicated constantly, using very subtle signals. They paid close attention to each other's body language, and were very good at reading intent as well as communicating it to each other. I asked Turid how much training went into Kenzie being able to read and respond to the gestures. She explained to me that all dogs innately knew how to read human gestures. I found this idea intriguing. We now have studies on street dogs that prove this to us and our school is in the process of conducting more studies to unravel more of this fascinating topic.

Watching Turid and Kenzie communicate, I felt that Nishi and I had been screaming at each other all these years. I was envious of what these two had, but I felt it was too late for Nishi and me to be able to talk like this. Kenzie must have come from a really good litter, and I imagined that the communication between Turid and Kenzie had been fine-tuned over years of laying the right foundation very early. I asked Turid about Kenzie's history and was shocked to learn that he had been abandoned at the vet, slated to be put down, and the vet decided to check with local 'dog lady' before going ahead with the euthanasia. 'Put down? What for? This is the most well-behaved dog I have ever seen. Who would ever want to put him down?' I asked her. She just shrugged.

By the time I visited Turid, I had worked with enough dogs with traumatic pasts, including my own girls Nishi and Cheerwal. I knew these dogs struggled to just trust humans, and such fine-tuned communication seemed far-fetched. I had to know what Turid had done to get Kenzie this far. She said, 'He asked to get on the sofa, and I told him that it was his house and his sofa and it was all okay.' That made no sense to me. What kind of a methodology was that, and how would that help me?

Over the next few days, I came to realize it was less of a *methodology* and more of a *philosophy*. It was a way of life based on mutual respect. Over the ten days that I stayed with her, I had several conversations with her, trying to translate this into something concrete I could do with my own dogs. Turid spoke extensively about giving dogs choices as critical to her way of life. She insisted that most of us try to push dogs to do too much. Turid never pushed Kenzie and paid very close attention to the most subtle signs Kenzie used to indicate his feelings. When Turid said that she helped Kenzie by letting him get on the sofa, what she was really saying was that she was letting him know that he had choices and control over his own life—or at least a significant part of it. Dogs with a traumatic past usually suffer from an intense sense of loss of control. What Turid was telling me was that she had helped Kenzie by demonstrating to him that he was in a place that he could call home and feel the right to at least be able to find a comfortable spot to curl up in and spend the evening.

One might imagine that a philosophy like this would lead Kenzie to be a spoilt brat. On the contrary, Kenzie was a calm dog who took wise decisions. He walked away from anything that might lead to stress or confrontation. Turid had learnt to watch his signals very carefully and would always respect his boundaries and limitations. He, in turn, respected hers. We were once having a snack when he walked up to us asking us if we would share. Turid did share some. Then, with the flick of her wrist and a quick movement of her eyes, she let him know that she was done sharing. He seemed to easily accept that and walked away. However, I must point out something here. While Turid let Kenzie know that she was done sharing, she did not command him to walk away. She was not telling him what she wanted him to do. She was telling him what *she* was not willing to do. He chose to respect her boundary and walked away. This subtle difference is the key to understanding Turid's relationship with her dog. Turid had put effort into building a relationship where she gave enough respect to Kenzie for him to want to return that respect. She never demanded it. She did not even train it into him. All of this was a lot for me to take in back then, and it took me years to process and fully understand what I had witnessed in Geithus.

As my stay with Turid came to an end, I knew that the relationship she had with Kenzie was what I wanted to have with Nishi and Cheerwal. My dogs had both been through hell in different ways. I had been desperately searching for what I could give to my dogs to compensate for what life had thrown at them. Now, I had my answer. I wanted to give them control over their lives. Who would have thought that it would boil down to something as basic as that! My ten days with Turid also made me realize that there was a lot more to Turid's way than just a few calming signals.

Mandal

After Geithus, two of Turid's students drove me down to the coastal town of Mandal. I was to stay with Agnes, helping her run a boarding facility for the next ten days.

The first morning in Mandal, Agnes drove me to her boarding facility. As the facility came into sight, Agnes pointed at the building and said, 'That's it.' Something did not quite sit right. There was a deathly silence. 'Do you not have too many dogs today?' I asked. '*Himmel og hav!* We are running past full capacity today,' she answered. Clearly, I needed to know what magic she was pulling off here and what *'Himmel og hav'* meant.

Agnes gave me a tour of the place and explained to me how they were managing to run a boarding facility with so many dogs in one building—yet with not a peep from the dogs. They understood that these dogs would all be very stressed because they were away from home, and their primary focus was to ensure that the dogs were kept in as stress-free an environment as possible, in their private rooms, with comfortable beds and water. Each of the dogs would get short walks with a lot of emphasis on sniffing, which calms dogs down. Some dogs were selected each day to do some more mentally stimulating activities, like nose games or enriched environment on a rotational basis. People were not allowed to approach the building by car and had to pull up a little way off and walk up, so as not to disturb the dogs. New dogs that were brought in were first taken into an external holding area, where they spent some time exploring and calming down.

Only after this were they brought into the main building. The humans were instructed to maintain pin-drop silence when inside the main building. It was indeed a pleasure to see how Agnes had taken Turid's ideas and applied them at her boarding facility.

Back home, there are not too many facilities that are run the way Agnes runs her boarding. I have already discussed how a boarding done badly can have undesired side-effects in dogs. So, now, when my students ask me where they can board their dogs, if they are unable to find a facility that keeps in mind a dog's stress levels, I encourage them to build a relationship with a pet-sitter. One must keep in mind that pet-sitters come with their own challenges. They are in our homes and often in a situation where there may not be anyone to oversee what they are doing. So we do need to take the necessary precautions, not only by working with trusted pet-sitters but also by spending enough time with them upfront to develop a gut feel about them—how they are around our dogs and how our dogs are around them. We should be able to trust our pet-sitters to be kind and responsible. We must conduct a similar assessment if we opt to use a boarding facility. Leaving our animals behind in the care of others needs to be done with care.

The Pulse Project

Heading back to Mandal, another interesting project Agnes wanted to talk to me about was the Pulse Project. For this, Agnes fashioned a device to measure the heart rate of a dog as they went along doing different activities.

The Pulse Project uncovered some fascinating stuff. Turid had taught us that dogs prefer to walk in a curve towards each other. Agnes showed us that when we walk straight up to a dog, it increases the heart rate of a dog significantly. However, if we walk in a curve there is only a minimal increase in heart rate, if at all. Similarly, bending over a dog increases their heart rate significantly, as does hugging. These are very valuable pieces of information, especially for people who are dealing with scared or reactive dogs. Things that make the pulse jump are best avoided with an unpredictable dog, because a jumping pulse means sudden SNS Activation, which can cause reactive dogs to bite, scared dogs to run away, and excited dogs to jump or bark.

The Pulse Project had more to contribute on the 'fetch' discussion Turid had started. Agnes showed how much the game of fetch increased a dog's heart rate, while sniffing decreased it. Agnes decided to demonstrate this last bit to me. We took her dog Odin to the study area and got him fitted with the equipment. Agnes scattered some treats for him to sniff out and, sure enough, his heart rate started dropping. We decided to try it again. This time, Agnes walked off to another room to hide treats. Odin stayed back but listened carefully to what Agnes was doing. As he stood listening, we noticed his heart rate drop further. Clearly, not just nose work, but other types of *brain-work* that involves thinking and concentrating can make the heart rate drop. This made me realize that while fetch can rile dogs up, *brain-work* can be used when we need dogs to calm down. The next leg of my trip was going to teach me exactly that.

UNDERSTANDING FETCH

'The Dog Pulse Project' demonstrated to me that activities like sniffing, listening, concentrating, thinking and strategizing typically slowed down the heart rate, while activities such as chasing after and fetching a stick or a ball increased their heart rate. Furthermore, the observations showed that the heart rate not only increased but got progressively higher each time.

A spike in heart rate means SNS Activation—an increase in adrenaline and, subsequently, in cortisol. In the essay on hyperactive dogs, I discuss at length how these 'micro' spikes can have a profound undesirable impact on the health and behaviour of the dog. Another problem with a game like fetch—played with a ball or a frisbee—is that it exposes the dog to possible injuries, which I will discuss at length in Chapter 8. That leads us to the question of why dogs engage in such activities in the first place and even seem so enthusiastic about them. The answer is the pain-numbing properties of SNS activation and the addictive properties of adrenaline. The pain-numbing properties of the hormones and neurotransmitters released during SNS activation help dogs keep up with us ignoring possible injuries. The addictive properties are what seem to bring them back over and over to these activities, coupled with our sense of excitement.

Fetch is often recommended as a remedy for behavioural problems or hyperactivity. It is described to be an activity that can help 'burn energy', but we know, from our own experience, that exercise has quite the opposite effect. After a workout in the morning we feel less 'burnt out' and more 'fired up' for the day ahead. This burst of energy is also perhaps why we cannot sleep for an hour or two after an exercise session if we work out at night. Even if the body is exhausted and not in a place to keep up, the mind refuses to shut down. This is the time the body requires to drain the additional cortisol. Moderate amounts of exercise with ample recovery time can be good for the body and mind. But over-exercising without paying heed to right posture and technique and without sufficient opportunity for the mind and body to rest and recover can not only get us wired up, but also have more dire long-term impact on cardiovascular health. It's during this time that dogs find it incredibly hard to cope and try to find outlets for this burst of energy. This might result in them destroying things, ripping things up, chewing things, barking excessively or running around in mad circles. Unfortunately, any kind of expression of this nature leads to more attempts to 'burn it out'. As you can imagine, this is a problem that keeps getting worse and worse, and in the process, puts the dog at a greater risk of injury.

Some clients wonder if some breeds were indeed not bred to retrieve. The answer is that they were bred to retrieve but not fetch. The Labrador Retriever and Golden Retriever do like to retrieve. With these dogs, we love to play search and retrieve games, where the dogs search for missing objects and then retrieve them. It involves the slow thinking process of searching, not frenzied running after an object.

There are many different and interesting ways to engage a dog's mind based on the dog's preference. Slow and deliberate games that involve sniffing, searching and strategizing not only help calm dogs down but also encourage them to use their minds. They will also not engage in movements that can hurt them. The Dog Pulse Project shows that these activities can bring down the heart rate, which means that the calming effect that they have can extinguish seemingly unrelated behavioural problems. The Internet today does have a lot of ideas for such thinking games. I, too, have added a book in my Recommended Books section. It can provide for hours of fun and bonding, without leaving the dog in a frenzy.

Kongsberg

At the end of ten days, Agnes bid me a teary goodbye after having helped me board a train to Kongsberg. I had been told by several people that the person I was going to meet next was very interesting. Anne Lill Kvam lived in Kongsberg and was generally considered the 'nose games' expert. She had trained dogs to sniff out landmines in Angola. She had to her credit a book and several DVDs on nose games. She had worked closely with Turid and, from what I had heard, was a bit of a genius.

As I got off at the Kongsberg train station, I looked around for a Shiba Inu. That was supposed to be how I recognized Anne Lill. I spotted the Shiba Inu, and at the other end of the leash was a lady dressed like she had walked out of the 70s, with a big grin planted on her face. She extended a warm welcome and introduced her dog as Fant. Fant did not seem very impressed with me, and I had by now learnt not to push dogs. So I maintained my distance.

The next morning, Anne Lill suggested that we take Fant out for *tracking*. Tracking is an exercise where one person pretends to be a lost victim and hides. The dog then searches for this victim based on their scent trail. Fant, however, was a pro and needed to be challenged, so we went to the woods in the morning and laid out a trail that Fant was to track later that day. We marked that trail with ribbons so that we wouldn't get lost and left behind a 'valuable object' at the end of the trail. Fant knew exactly what he had been brought there to do. He was to track our scent trail from earlier and find the 'valuable object' that we pretended we had lost on the trail. He started out on the trail, but suddenly he seemed to veer off on the wrong track. We wondered why he had done that, until we realized that I had managed to pollute the trail by walking back on it. Fant had not veered off, he had simply found the fresher trail and taken the shortcut!

Fant constantly amused us with his seeming lack of a sense of humour. He was an intense guy. I realized later that he did not lack humour, he just had a dry sense of it. He eventually did warm up to me, and it felt very special because

I was apparently one of only five people he liked in the whole world. He did, however, love Anne Lill deeply and was very thoughtful about her. Anne Lill told me of her story, where during one of her walks in the woods, she found a chanterelle mushroom and squealed in joy. Fant noticed how happy it made her. The thoughtful loving gentleman that he was, he decided to make her happier. Every time his snout detected chanterelle mushrooms, he would lead her to them, just to see her happy. Just like that, he had taught himself to sniff out mushrooms for her.

By the time I was in Kongsberg, it was beginning to get cold. I was staying in a trailer on a campsite. The campsite was dreary, so I would spend most of my time in Anne Lill's cosy little home, in front of the fire. One such evening, she decided to show me how Fant could differentiate between scents. She pulled out two tea bags and asked me to watch how he could tell the difference between the hibiscus tea and jasmine tea. He seemed to get it wrong. Yet again, I realized I had set it up all wrong and managed to use two hibiscus tea bags instead of one jasmine and one hibiscus. Despite that, Fant could tell the difference between the two hibiscus tea bags too—picking the one Anne Lill had touched. A dog's nose is truly remarkable.

Unlike Turid, who had stopped training her dogs, Anne Lill did train hers to engage in sniffing games. However, she warned me repeatedly about overdoing it. Sniffing is a very tiring activity for dogs. Just because they are good at it does not mean that that is all they want to do. A dog needs more to make their life meaningful. A dog is a hyper-social animal and requires good social contact. Like any other animal, they too value their freedom and will appreciate choice in whatever aspects of life they can control. Turid would repeat to her students, over and over and over—choices, mental stimulation and social contact!

I had always known that dogs needed mental stimulation, but I had got it all wrong. To provide mental stimulation, I had started to train Nishi and Cheerwal to do a few tricks, but it was in Norway that I realized the true potential of a dog's mind. I watched the relationship between Turid and Kenzie, Agnes and Odin, Anne Lill and Fant. These relationships were rich and meaningful. The dogs were being given a lot of freedom and responsibility. The dogs were being trusted to make good decisions, and they did. They were engaging their strongest faculty, their nose, in very meaningful and enjoyable ways. Compared to what they were doing, the trick-training I was asking my dogs to do seemed to be a repetitive production-line job that would never come close to being as gratifying as jobs that allow us to play to our strengths, but done in moderation and in balance with other aspects of living.

I thought I was going to Norway to learn as much as I could. Instead, I had to unlearn. Unlearning is difficult. My unlearning involved tears, brutal honesty and humility. Norway changed my life. There was no going back!

CHAPTER 6

THE LIVES OF STREETIES

Streeties

It is hard to be a dog lover in India and not talk about street dogs, or streeties, as we like to call them. They are typically mixed-breed dogs—a mix of our aboriginal breeds and several popular foreign breeds brought to India over the last several hundred years. These dogs are everywhere, are not really owned by anyone, and are mostly friendly and harmless. They are free-ranging dogs and act out of free will. They are not confined in any way and are not trained by anyone. To me, this makes them the perfect dogs to study to really know what dogs are like. We have seen repeatedly that studies on captive animals or animals in labs do not give us the full picture. In my opinion, these dogs will play a critical role in improving our understanding of dogs in the years to come. Before we attempt to understand them better, it is perhaps time to take a step back and understand dogs as a species, their evolution and how they came to be what they are.

DOG EVOLUTION

We must start at the beginning. Where do dogs come from and when did it all begin?

Initially, evolutionists believed that the origin of dogs dates back to 15,000 years ago, when humans were predominantly agriculturists. During this phase of human evolution, domestication of animals seemed to have been the trend. Several animals were domesticated during this period and the dog was considered to be a part of a similar endeavour by mankind. In recent years, the view has changed after the discovery of several fossil evidences that date the existence of dogs to 20,000–30,000 years ago. I will not be surprised if we unearth older fossils. Some evolutionists use DNA evidence to say the dog story goes back to as long as 1,30,000 years ago.

While the debate is ongoing in academic circles, there seems to be consensus on a few things: that the origin of dogs goes further back than we had earlier imagined, well into the time when humans were still hunter-gatherers, and that the dog is not a product of domestication by humans, but a product of co-evolution with humans.

The common misconception is that dogs evolved from modern-day wolves. The newer theory is that dogs and modern-day wolves are likely to have shared a common ancestor, while some argue that there may have been more than one prehistoric canid that led to the modern-day dog. For the sake of this discussion, let's simplify this and call these animals 'proto-dogs'. Evolution is a process by which animals become specialized, becoming more efficient at utilizing certain resources so as to give them a survival advantage—perhaps in the form of a novel food source or an effective defence mechanism. Experts now believe that the more curious of the proto-dogs, who were fearless enough to approach *Homo sapiens*, started specializing in using human resources to give themselves a survival advantage. This led to the creation of the species *Canis familiaris*, a.k.a. the Dog. Some of the remaining may have gone on to become *Canis lupus* or the Wolf, a dog's closest living relative in modern times.

Folklore and pop-culture often portray wolves as the more fearless of the canids. However, a single encounter with them will confirm beyond question that dogs are indeed the more curious and fearless ones. Back when I was in Norway, I had the unique opportunity of visiting a wolf conservation park with Anne Lill Kvam. The wolves lived in a massive wooded area, and we only had access to a distant observation deck. I happened to catch a glimpse of a few of them, only because they had been lured out for feeding. They disappeared very quickly, reaffirming how shy of humans they really are. These wolves, of course, had very limited human contact, so one can expect this level of wariness from a *wild animal*. However, in another large enclosure, there were *socialized wolves*, who had been raised by human beings since birth. Anne Lill was familiar with one of the older wolves. She graciously agreed to introduce me to him, who, she claimed would recognize her. These wolves, too, were in a protected wooded area. We had to make our presence known and wait for them to emerge. We spent almost half an hour calling out to them. I started to wonder if any of them even recognized Anne Lill. Eventually, our patience was rewarded by a pair of intense icy-blue eyes staring back at us from the woods. This was followed by a few more pairs of eyes and a few juveniles slowly popping their heads out. Anne Lill continued trying to call out to the one wolf she knew, until eventually he emerged. Once he emerged, he did seem to recognize her, and his body language suddenly changed. I saw the happy doggy-like-playfulness that we have come to associate with the sign of a dog recognizing a human. This is in sharp contrast with my experience with Kajal, a street dog, who started recognizing me after just two interactions. From then on, she would respond to the sound of my bicycle approaching and come bounding up to me. She definitely did not need as much coaxing as these wolves did. Street dogs, unlike these wolves, are fearless to the point of being willing to approach random strangers at the first sight of friendliness.

Given the ubiquity of dogs around humans, it seems understandable that we take this extreme fearlessness of dogs for granted and don't really notice the oddity of this behaviour in the animal kingdom. Consider this: Yuval Noah Harari, in his book *Sapiens*, exposes the disturbing parallel in the timelines and geographies of the genesis and spread of *Homo sapiens*, and the extension of most contemporary megafauna. He discusses how the only large animals that seemed to have survived the wake of humans are the ones who learnt to be wary of humans. Understandably, the golden rule in the undomesticated animal kingdom seems to be the one articulated so well by Sher Khan in *The Jungle Book*: 'Man is forbidden!'

Wolf evolution, too, seems to have used this winning strategy of wariness to produce one of the very few megafauna species to have survived, but dog evolution seems to have used the opposite strategy to create a far more successful species. While humans bred wariness out of all domestic species, dogs seem to have gotten there on their own.

Throughout the history of humankind, dogs have always found a way to make themselves useful to us. When humans were nomads, dogs alerted them about intruders such as wild animals; when we were hunters, dogs aided in hunting; when we became farmers, dogs helped by hunting rats and other vermin that destroyed the produce; when we started owning property, dogs guarded it; and when we moved to urban settings that are stressful, dogs helped in reducing stress. In the age of loneliness, dogs seem to be offering friendship. It seems that dogs don't serve a single purpose, but are versatile enough to do many things, depending on the changing needs of the people around them.

Thus, the one true survival advantage of dogs seems to be their unique ability to be better collaborators with people than any other species. Understandably, their primary preoccupation seems to be our happiness, and their survival strategy seems to be to do anything to make humans happy. While this is not as visually dramatic as the tall neck of a giraffe or the hard shell of a turtle or the long snout of an anteater, it is still an adaptation that is distinctly noticeable in several aspects of a dog, including social structure, communication, looks, diet and mental makeup.

1. To make us happy, dogs need to be able to read our emotions very well. They indeed are master navigators of our emotions. One study shows that when dogs look at our faces, they preferentially look at the right side, because humans tend to emote more on that side. Humans, of course, without being aware of this, also tend to look at the right side of the face of the person they are speaking with, because we do value emotion as an integral component of communication and maintaining social decorum. This ability to read human emotion so keenly is not even seen in

other primates. However, dogs do it. Can dogs smell fear? Studies suggest they can. Contrary to the popular belief that dogs react to fear with aggression, they actually respond to our fear by getting scared themselves. They detect and react to other emotions too. For instance, they respond to our sorrow with concern and our joy is mirrored as joy in them. Another study shows that dogs can not only read emotions expressed on our faces, but also in the photographs of our faces. The study goes on to show that dogs can recognize emotions in the photographs of our full face as well as photographs of half of our faces that reveal only either our eyes or lips. Simply put, you cannot fake a smile in front of a dog because they can see it is not reflected in your eyes.

2. **Theory of Mind** is defined as the ability to understand that others have desires and intentions that are different from ours, and our attempt to understand those. For example, if a student in class looked at her watch, I am not only going to realize that the action is associated with some thoughts in her mind, but I am also going to try and determine what those thoughts might be. While anthropologists agree that this is a strong human trait, ethologists continue to debate about how many animals seem to exhibit

theory of mind. However, several experts believe that dogs seem to do extremely well when it comes to human beings. Several articles on the concept cite the example of dogs as having a unique interspecies ability for this particular skill. This was, of course, demonstrated in a fascinating experiment conducted by Duke University. It involved placing two cups in front of an animal, hiding food under one of the cups and then pointing to where the food actually was. Of course, for most dog owners, it is not at all surprising that if you point in the direction where the food is placed, the dog very quickly learns what you are pointing at and happily accepts your help to discover food. The Duke University experiment interestingly showed that while this is a skill we take for granted in dogs, it seems to be non-existent in their cousins, the wolves, as well as in our own cousins, chimpanzees and bonobos. Another interesting study conducted on street dogs shows that dogs are good at not only taking directions from us but also quickly determining if we are helpful or unhelpful people, and using that information to decide if they would like to take our help or reject it altogether. In other words, they are judging us as honest/dishonest people.

3. Dogs also exhibit a unique ability for extreme physical adaptation. They seem to be present in all climates and all geographies in which human beings are present, ranging from Innuit dogs and Laikas in the snowy regions to the Salukis in the scorching heat of the deserts.

4. Dogs are brilliant at communicating with us, as demonstrated by their extensive use of facial expressions that are easy to recognise. Moreover, dogs also seem to vocalize far more than wolves. This is postulated to be a direct result of the fact that human beings respond better to vocal cues compared to visual signals. Thanks to Turid, we now have knowledge of calming signals that we can use to understand our dogs, but even without such formal documentation, most of us intuitively understand dogs. There is a little bakery right outside my house, where I often see people buying a little snack to feed the street dogs that choose to hang out around the bakery. I once asked a man who had just bought a packet of biscuits and fed them to a streety if he had a dog of his own. He shook his head vehemently and said he did not have dogs of his own and did not even consider himself a dog lover. I then asked him, why he had chosen to buy biscuits for the street dogs. He looked confused, shrugged his shoulders and said, 'Because he

asked me.' I asked him how he knew that the dog had 'asked him', to which he obviously did not have an answer. He just stared at me like I had lost my mind, shrugged his shoulders and just repeated, 'He asked. What do you mean "how"?' I am quite sure the man had not read Turid's books or had any academic knowledge of how dogs communicate. Yet, it seems that the dog and the man had no communication barrier whatsoever.

5. Wolves are pack animals. They are masters at communicating with each other because being pack animals allows them to hunt better. Dogs, however, are not strictly pack animals. They seem to use pack-like structures when defending themselves. However, when looking for food, they seem to prefer doing it alone or in pairs. It seems that their highly flexible social structure is driven by human preference. If you imagine a pack of street dogs sitting outside the bakery or heading towards it, you can easily see how the people there would not only hesitate to feed the pack but also feel intimidated and run away or chase the pack away. However, a lone dog hanging out by the bakery seems to be far less intimidating, far more vulnerable-looking and far more endearing—increasing the odds of humans helping them out.

6. What I find most fascinating is that dogs seem to have a unique ability to make us fall in love with them and care for them as if they were our own young—for no reason other than love itself. There are ample studies to show that eye contact and physical contact with dogs generate oxytocin (the love hormone) and endorphins (happy hormones) in us. Clearly, they are not in cahoots with cupid. So how do dogs make us fall in love? The answer could be 'neoteny'. Neoteny is simply a fancy way of saying that dogs just refuse to grow up and, therefore, end up being very endearing to us. They are even supposed to have extra muscles in their eyes that help them create that highly endearing wide-eyed 'puppy-dog' look. We associate big eyes with infants and are automatically drawn to it. Several studies are currently trying to understand why, while most animals stop playing once they pass their juvenile age, dogs continue to play intensely well into their adulthood. Many dogs even play in their old age, as long as their bodies can keep up. Is this because their play makes them more endearing to us? While the jury is still out on this, one thing seems certain. What dogs are today makes it almost impossible not to fall in love with them. And that is what makes dogs so interesting to me.

Kermit

One fine evening in Bangalore, a gorgeous streety appeared outside my house. She seemed curious about me, but not quite willing to accept any physical contact. I tried offering her some food in a bid to see her more often. Before I knew it, I had become her dedicated feeder. I named her Kermit. Every evening, I would step out during our feeding time, looking for her. She would diligently be waiting for me, maintaining a respectable distance and demanding that of me too. I had to put the food out and step away, allowing her to eat in peace. I spent some time getting to know her and gaining her trust through polite interactions, until she eventually rewarded me with permission to touch her.

One day, as Kermit was eating the food I had put out for her, something caught her attention. She stopped eating, took a few steps back and started staring down the street. It was dark, and I could not see what she was looking at. A few seconds later, her excitement increased. She was now doing a little dance and making a whining sound. The sound seemed to have attracted another dog, and he deliberately walked up to her. She seemed terribly excited by his presence. She stepped away from her food almost as if she was offering it up to him. He gladly accepted the offer and ate the food. Clearly, they were friends. I named him Crowley and watched them share several meals.

Street dogs are often pictured to be fighting with each other in an attempt at survival of the fittest. We are used to the 'dog eat dog' metaphor, but that was not what I was seeing. I was looking at a dog who did not have access to unlimited resources, who knew that she had to eat when she found food, and yet was willing to share valuable meaty food with another dog.

One might wonder if she felt bullied to give it up, but something happened a few days later that told me that what I had witnessed was not bullying, it was friendship. Like it often happens among friends, something went sour between the two a few days later. When Kermit was eating, Crowley approached as usual. His body language was the first clue. Something was off between them. He walked up to her gingerly. Instead of sharing her meal, she snapped at him. They got into a shouting match and he backed off. She was not interested in sharing. For several weeks after, Crowley would lurk in the background, some days trying to convince her and on other days trying to demand. She was having none of it.

Kermit and Crowley had a constantly changing dynamic, exhibited clearly by their body language. A few weeks after their spat, they seemed to have made up and were sharing again. Kermit and Crowley got me hooked to the idea of wanting to study more street dogs. While a dog's interaction with humans is fascinating, what these two showed me was that their own lives were far more interesting than I had previously noticed. I knew I wanted to study them, but I was not sure where to start.

Genesis of the Study

I bonded with Kermit before I left for Norway in 2013. In Norway, Turid and I were discussing how much dogs need to move and exercise. That gave me an idea. Animals, in general, can gauge the optimal movement for them. A tiger or a bear does not need to be reminded to get their twenty minutes of cardio. The same is the case with streeties. They just know how much they need to move. Kermit and Crowley definitely did. I figured that if I could determine how much Kermit moved and how she exercised, it might give me an idea of the optimal movement for dogs. So, once I returned, I started studying Kermit by attempting to follow her. But quickly I realized that streeties do not like to be followed and are very good at 'shaking off a tail'. So I had to re-imagine the study and altered it to instead observe small durations of behaviour spread across a large collection of dogs. The study lasted four years and included more than 700 observations. The findings of the study are detailed in the essay at the end of this chapter.

'Lives of Streeties' started out in 2014 as a quantitative study of the activity budget of dogs. After its initial presentation, the project took on a new shape. During my observations, I came to befriend many of these dogs and saw that their lives were so rich in social interactions, emotions and just plain drama that their stories had to be told. It was important to not only dispel myths about streeties but also better understand dogs in general. Consequently, the project took on a new avatar, to chronicle the stories of the lives of streeties. In the rest of this chapter, I will share some of those stories with you, covering different aspects of a dog's life when left to their own free will.

Sleep

A streety's favourite activity by far is sleeping, and dogs seem to get incredibly creative about finding comfy beds. For this project, I went online and asked people to send me pictures of streeties sleeping. These pictures made for very hilarious viewing. They were found sleeping on top of cars, on the landings of stairs that ran outside homes and in front of offices, inside parked auto-rickshaws, on top of motorbikes, and even on the rooftops of homes that did not chase them away. It is not uncommon to see several dogs sleeping in close proximity to each other. Turid claims that dogs are 'social sleepers', which makes sense in their context, because it seems that sleeping together means that they can take turns to keep a lookout. Streeties are also not den animals, contrary to popular belief. The sleeping preferences of streeties are functionally driven. If a streety is unwell or whelping, they may hide in drains. On hot afternoons or rainy days, some may be seen sleeping under cars. On cold days, holes and sand piles seem to give them warmth, and they can be seen sleeping closer to each other. Many seem to love sleeping on elevated surfaces like on top of sand piles, staircase landings and even on top of parked cars. Sometimes, they encounter generous humans who permit them to sleep within their home or office premises and offer them a bedding surface.

Streety Guardians

Many of our streeties seem to have guardians. One such guardian that stands out in my mind is Yellamma. Yellamma stays close to my house, in a tiny hut. Two dogs live right outside her hut. I spoke to her about them, and she said she had named them Caesar and PV. She spoke affectionately about feeding them and caring for them. She said she saved up money to buy them chicken once a week. She proudly claimed that she provided for their healthcare—when they needed it and to the extent she could afford. At one end of the spectrum of human generosity are people like Yellamma. At the other end is the work of people like Bismi. Bismi works for a software company in Bangalore. At the end of each workday, she makes food for more than a hundred dogs, carries it out in large vats and feeds her regulars. She knows every one of them by name and takes care of their health. While she does solicit donations at times, most of this is largely self-funded.

Bismi and Yellamma are not the only people of their kind in Bangalore. They do not 'own' these dogs, but care for each of them immensely. They understand the perils of a streety's life and know that any day, any of these dogs may turn up with grave injuries or not turn up at all. Giving your heart to a dog under such circumstances is a brave thing to do. Once you start caring for a dog, it is very tempting to take them home and shield them from the harsh conditions they live in, but it is not possible to take home tens or hundreds of dogs. Many streeties also fiercely guard their independence and do not want to move into homes. So, people like Bismi and Yellamma risk severe heartbreak and continue to care for these streeties, all the while respecting these dogs' autonomy and freedom.

Food

Some streeties are lucky to find themselves patrons like Yellamma or Bismi. Some others find establishments like bakeries and restaurants that do not chase them away. These dogs seem to know exactly when to visit these establishments. Bakeries or tea shops, it seems, are best visited during afternoon hours when cab drivers arrive there for lunch or tea. Fancier restaurants and butchers are ideal to visit at night, during closing hours, when the garbage is being taken out. They wait patiently, working their charm to convince people to either buy them some snacks or feed them the leftovers. To my pleasant surprise, there really is not a dearth of people who are willing to oblige a streety begging for food. However, the problem is that we simply have far too many dogs for the resources available. Resource crunches lead to poor health and increased stress in streeties, which in turn results in an increase of unhealthy dog population, resulting in conflict—both among dogs and between humans and dogs.

I had another interesting observation about the dietary habits of dogs. When we talk about dogs, we often conjure up a picture of a fierce predator hunting frequently. Throughout the course of my study—and quite frankly, throughout my life around street dogs—I have not really seen a street dog hunt. I've heard about it, and I believe some do, especially the ones on the fringes of cities, towns, villages and forests, but within cities and towns, it's a lot more common to find streeties scavenging than it is to see them hunting. The most common sight is to see them begging. Interestingly, many of these dogs frequently settle for dal and rice over protein-rich food like a rodent or a bird. When I drive past the slums of Ejipura, I see goats and streeties playing with each other, and the image of the savage predator just melts away. Most streeties are no different from our pet dogs, in this regard, preferring to use their charming eyes to beg for our food, rather than to go out and hunt. Goats, apparently, are 'friends and not food'!

Social Interactions

For me, the most fascinating part about street dogs is their
rich and complex social interactions. When I talk about social
interactions, I must talk about Kajal. Kajal was a dainty, petite
black dog who one day turned up on my study route. At the
time, I had a rule that I would not befriend any dog on my
route because I worried about influencing their activities that
I was trying to study. But Kajal insisted on getting to know
me, and I was left with no choice but to think of an alternate
way of proceeding with my study.

During the course of my study, I got to know the different
members of Kajal's group. There was Kajal, of course, the
protagonist of our story and the most fun member of the
group. Then there was Poppy, the group geriatric. He was
the oldest member, partially blind, and seemed to basically
be humoured by the rest of the group. He was left to stick
to the routines he was used to. There was Goldilocks, a new
mum who generally stayed a little away from the group. There
were also a bunch of young, rowdy, male dogs who were part
of this group. One day, when I went to see them, I noticed
a huge male dog there. He was taller than most streeties, had
a strong, square face and seemed to be very healthy. I named
him Ken. Kajal and Ken seemed to be communicating with
each other quite intensely. As I watched them, I realized that
I was watching romance unfurl. I watched Kajal give Ken coy
looks and tease him. She would turn and look at him, then
walk away a few steps, and he would follow her. They would
explore things together. A study on these dogs shows that

during the monsoons they go into heat, and are more likely to be found exploring in pairs. It was indeed the monsoons when Kajal and Ken's romance began.

A few days later, the group had decided that Ken was not meant to be Kajal's suitor. One morning, when I visited them, I saw that they were in the middle of banishing Ken from the group. Kajal seemed to strut in and out of this drama, rather aware that all the fuss was about her. The other female members chose to stay away. The young male members were growling and posturing, edging the much bigger Ken to slowly back out of the group. They were taking a protective stance towards Kajal, or perhaps a possessive one. Poppy was contributing to this whole drama by growling, but not exactly orienting his growl towards Ken. He seemed to have lost the point altogether, but seemed to just want to have his two cents in. The entire interaction involved not a modicum of actual violence. I could have watched this forever, but I knew that I needed to do the right thing, and whisked Kajal away to be spayed. If tensions kept mounting, one of the dogs may have ended up hurting another dog, which would make the humans in the neighbourhood nervous. Once Kajal was spayed, the group shrunk in size.

Kajal's drama revealed to me interesting details about social structures of dogs and the dynamics of dog groups. Wolves are considered pack animals. A pack is a stable group of related members. By this definition, it looks like streety groups cannot really be called packs. Kajal's group was not composed of related members. It was definitely not stable—

growing from three to thirteen in size and then shrinking down to three. The role of the group members was rather interesting too. There was no clear leader of any kind. Poppy seemed to be the group elder who felt like he had to have a say; he was humoured by the rest but not really taken too seriously. There were a few people who fed these dogs, but Poppy was used to eating at one particular house, and he ate first. There was one spot that he liked to sleep in. Kajal behaved like a happy, irresponsible, flirty, fun teenager. Goldilocks was preoccupied with her puppies, and when it came to their survival, she called the shots. She seemed to have few opinions, but when she did, others simply respected them, no questions asked. Ken was Kajal's boyfriend, who was the latest addition to the group. He was the biggest of them all and it seemed for a while that he was going to be Kajal's mate, until he was banished from the group. After the young members banished Ken, it was not evident which one was going to get to mate with Kajal or if there would be more than one of them. While wolves are known to be monogamous, dogs are promiscuous. More than one male can mate with a female dog and end up impregnating her. Essentially, Kajal's family had a complex and nuanced social structure, much like a joint family.

The groups that dogs formed also seemed to have fluid rules on membership. While the groups allowed some members to join, they refused entry to a few others. A few years later, I observed another group, consisting of Pops, the dad; Red, the mum; and Flashy, Loco and Coco, the puppies. Red looked very young and was perhaps a juvenile herself.

Turid would often say that dogs were not ready to be parents until they were at least twenty-four months old, and that definitely seemed the case with Red. She was mostly absent, but Pops was a brilliant father and just a wonderful dog. He took great care of his puppies and allowed a few other dogs to join his group. The older, more unwell dogs seemed incapable of taking care of themselves. When faced with a threat, it was always Pops who stood up for his entire group, supported by some of the other younger dogs. Once, he let a young dog, Fluffy, into his group. Fluffy was a bit of an obnoxious dog, frequently picking fights with the puppies. Eventually, Pops banished Fluffy from his group.

Streeties also share interesting dynamics with dogs of neighbouring groups. When dogs cross territory lines, some trespassers are tolerated more than others. Dogs of neighbouring groups also seem to have working alliances, where a few young dogs from neighbouring groups team up together late at night to go looking for food or exploring new territory. Some dogs choose to be part of groups. Some prefer to be loners. Almost none of these preferences seems to be set in stone. Given my observations, I realized that while we now do seem to have a better understanding of the social structure of wolves, it would be a grave mistake to assume that dogs have the exact same kind of social setups. Dogs are a species by themselves and need to be given due attention.

Conflict Resolution

Kajal and Ken's story showed me how remarkable dogs were at conflict resolution. I got to witness this on another occasion during my study, early one morning. As I went out on my beat, I noticed eight dogs, standing still like statues, seemingly staring at a wall. This piqued my curiosity, and I walked towards them. Then, as I continued to observe, one by one, each of the dogs started to trot purposefully towards a grassy patch on my right. The dogs seemed to want to go sniff the patch and aimlessly look around. This sudden change from being hyper-focused on the wall to aimlessly lingering on a grassy patch made no sense to me. If that was not confusing enough, all the dogs suddenly lost interest in the grassy patch and trotted off to my left, just as purposefully as they had gone to the patch. Something was afoot, but what? I tried to get closer to the grassy patch to get to the bottom of this strange behaviour. I then heard barking at a distance, and I realized what I had just witnessed. The barking dogs were Caesar and PV. The dogs that were exhibiting the strange behaviour were perhaps just passing by—tourist dogs. Caesar and PV felt that the tourists had gotten too close to their property and were issuing fair warning. On hearing the barks, the tourists first froze, then moved closer so that they were well within the line of sight of Caesar and PV. Here, they spent some time, most likely giving calming signals to Caesar and PV to indicate that they intended no confrontation. There was sniffing, paw lifts, head turns and body turns. When they felt the message had been adequately communicated, they decided to carry on and walked away.

Turid had, on several occasions, taught us that dogs were very effective at using calming signals to avoid conflict. 'The language of dogs is the language of peace,' she would tell us. My observations were showing me what she meant and helping me gain a new appreciation for these remarkable creatures, who are so often misunderstood. Street dogs are often associated with stereotypes such as vicious behaviour, engaged in constant conflict with each other, and unsafe for humans and livestock. Every time I hear views like these, my mind goes straight back to the dogs and goats of the Ejipura slum frolicking together. During their courtship, I had also seen Kajal and Ken easily strut past a family of pigs, casually tossing a calming signal their way. In all my observations, I could not capture a single instance of a streety attacking a person, dog or any other animal.

This is not to suggest that conflicts never happen. They do on occasion and are often poorly reported to make it look like the norm, instead of the anomaly they truly are. As expected, such reporting evokes strong emotions, some people coming down on the side of humans, some on the side of dogs, and some on the side of other animals that may be involved in the conflict. Irrespective of their stance, the one thing everyone agrees on is that any amount of conflict causes damage to all parties involved. However, the country remains deeply divided on how to address the issue. There seems to be a lack of will on the part of civic authorities to take a well-informed, balanced approach. Awareness and education are not even on the radar of policymakers. However, it is heartening to see that citizens and dog lovers do frequently take it upon themselves to identify and implement solutions. An effective partnership between the streety guardians of the country and the willing civic bodies will make the biggest impact in this regard, and such partnerships are already taking shape. It is an uphill battle, but not a hopeless one.

The Midnight Prowl

Feeding streeties has an interesting consequence on the behaviours of these dogs. Kajal's group seems to have found patrons. They were all well fed and cared for. The group had also been allowed to sleep at a construction site. The tarp used to cover the construction material provided cosy spots for them to sleep in. I called this site Hotel Canine. When I drove past it, most nights, the dogs did not wake up unless I stopped and called them out. In the beginning, when I did that, they'd come out and bark at me for a few minutes, and then head back to their warm beds. Once they got to know me better, apart from Kajal, none of the others were really interested in even getting up. Their full bellies seemed to make them reluctant to be too active and give up the comfort of their warm beds.

Two roads down, the scene was very different. Handa and gang had no patrons. They were on their own. Each night, they seemed to utilize the thin traffic to set out looking for food. They were likely to be rather hungry and charged up. I once saw one of them chase a motorbike, which struck me as interesting. Bangaloreans on motorbikes are all too familiar with dogs chasing after them at night, so I had imagined I'd see all the streeties up and about, being complete nuisances at night. But that was not really the case. Most dogs that were taken care of couldn't care less and wanted to sleep through the night. The dogs that were hungry, ill or terrified stayed up, barked all night and chased bikes. When people contact me, asking me for help with their streeties chasing bikes, I often ask them to make note of the time this happens and suggest they feed the dog just before that time of the day. Of course, one also needs to consider the health of the dogs, because often, those that are starting to fall ill or experience joint pain or discomfort take to chasing bikes. While it is hard to really nail down what triggers these behaviours in streeties, and almost impossible to train them, it may be possible to alter behaviours by tending to their health and food. Several streety guardians use tools of this kind to keep their dogs from getting into trouble. Care is a big part of understanding and altering streety behaviours, especially when it comes to human–dog conflict.

HUMAN–STREETY CONFLICT

One solution to any human–animal conflict is to get rid of the animals. But there are believed to be more than 200 million free-ranging dogs in the world, and it would be foolish to think that getting rid of all of them is going to have no consequences. After all, cities are urban ecosystems in and of themselves, and dogs have lived alongside humans in such ecosystems for millennia. History is replete with evidence that drastic and dramatic alterations of ecosystems by mass killings almost always have unforeseen and undesirable side effects.

Dr S. Chinni Krishna argues that like all ecosystems, urban ecosystems too have a holding capacity, or the ability of the ecosystem to support life. If we erase one form of life, another may take its place, which may bring its own problems. Dog populations may be replaced by rat populations, which can then pose some severe problems for humans. Unlike dogs, rats cannot be caught and vaccinated, and unlike dogs, rats can find their way into our homes with the ability to contaminate our food and water.

Consider the following examples from an article from The Animal People Forum:

- Fiji, Taiwan and Malaysia saw leptospirosis outbreaks after mass destruction of street dogs.
- China saw a similar increase after mass killing of snakes.
- Closer home, the 1994 plague outbreak in Surat is believed to have been an indirect effect of the mass killing of dogs.
- In Marseille, France, a study ties increased leptospirosis after rains to rats. One can only speculate how a country like India may be impacted with increased rat populations.
- China, which is supposed to be much better at destroying its street dog population, still reports a million cases of leptospirosis annually. India reports less than 10,000, and while this is perhaps a gross misrepresentation, it indicates that the

dogs of India may in fact be playing a role that needs to be better understood before we go on a killing spree.

In addition to the issue of rats, there is another phenomenon we are likely to observe in the aftermath of killing of street dogs. Mass killing can shape the behaviours of entire populations. At a conference in Rome in 2019, we were presented with a case study from Morocco of a stable and friendly population of 200 street dogs in a specific neighbourhood. The entire population was shot down in 2018, but by the next season, this old friendly population of 200 had been replaced with a less friendly population of 700. Killing programmes typically end up catching or killing dogs that are the most friendly and the least wary of humans. The dogs that survive are likely to be the ones that are more wary and more fearful. Thus, we are placing an evolutionary pressure on the dog population and beginning to shape them to be more wary and, in turn, making them more aggressive towards people. Epigenetics may explain the transmission of this fear across generations.

Irrespective of the mechanics of it, it is not hard to understand that persecuted animal populations grow wary of humans. Over the past few years, I have been exchanging notes with people from different parts of the world that have free-ranging dogs, and the pattern is evident: persecuted free-ranging dogs are wary of humans and more likely to get into conflict with them, while free-ranging dogs in cities such Bangalore are incorrigibly friendly.

In 1964, Blue Cross India studied this issue further, and it was revealed that the Madras Corporation had been running an unsuccessful catch-and-kill programme for over a hundred years. The programme was eventually replaced after the Blue Cross study revealed its ineffectiveness.

What then is the solution to addressing human–dog conflict? Interestingly, the answer may already be right in front of us. With a little understanding of dogs, it might be possible to set up an environment that is not conducive for conflict. Consider these examples:

- In the Nilgiris, the street dog population was stabilized and rabies eradicated by the Worldwide Veterinary Service, India.
- Help in Suffering (India) managed to bring down the incidences of rabies to zero in the places that they were operating between 1994 and 2002, whilst the incidences of rabies in other parts of the city were actually rising.
- Blue Cross had far more success with its ABC programme than the Madras Corporation had with its mass-killing programme.
- Mission Rabies managed to achieve zero human rabies deaths in Goa by working on a rigorous vaccination drive from 2013 to 2018.

Apart from these, there are examples closer still from which we can observe and learn—streety guardians. The country has a network of several people who take care of one or several groups of streeties and do it in a very responsible way. These people are committed to reducing human–dog conflict because they understand that the first sign of conflict often results in the dogs being killed. Thanks to social media, there is extensive knowledge-sharing among many of them. A structured study of their best practices is definitely warranted, but I will summarize what I understand from them in the rest of the essay.

The first thing to do is to stabilize the population, which can be achieved by Animal Birth Control (ABC). In India, this is expected to be provided by the government, but a partnership with citizens can go a long way in identifying the dogs that need it and getting them to and back from ABC centres. Once ABC is done, the population remains more or less stable for about ten to fifteen years. Dogs are territorial animals, which means that these dogs will not allow new dogs to join their group, giving us a known set of dogs to work with and giving us ample time to do so.

The next part is to influence their behaviour. Dogs are generally happy, silly animals, and it takes as little as good health to keep them in a good mood. Happy dogs rarely bite. Indian streeties are also very hardy animals that are easy to keep healthy. Basic vaccinations are also provided by civic bodies in India, and citizen groups can organize vaccination drives in their neighbourhoods. Large cities in India have a growing number of independent rescuers who can help in providing timely medical care in case of accidents and injuries. Social media makes it easier to reach out to these rescuers. A full belly goes a long way in making the dogs happy and maybe even a bit lazy, making them less inclined to get into any conflict. Picture the fat dog outside the bakery, and it's hard to imagine him being interested in engaging in any fights. Dogs have evolved to be able to digest most of what we eat, making it quite easy for us to feed them. No special meals are required either.

Once we have achieved a stable, healthy population, we must educate ourselves and our children on basic safety around animals (dogs are no different here). Children tend to be the most vulnerable around animals because they tend to be loud, unpredictable and not as cautious as they need to be. While both adults and children can make mistakes in their interaction with animals, children pay a bigger price because of their size and because their faces are too close to the animals' face during bad interactions. The following is my list of top four suggestions to keep ourselves safe around animals:

1. Never approach any animal head on. Invite the animal and wait for them to approach. If the

animal chooses not to, let them be. Do *not* chase after animals—ever.

2. Stay away from eating, sleeping, unwell/injured, lactating and confined animals (animals in cages or tied animals). These animals can get easily stressed and have unpredictable reactions. Contact professionals or rescuers if such an animal needs help.

3. Never hug an animal. Never interact with an animal in a way that restricts its movement or makes it feel trapped. If such animals end up biting, the child's face and neck are too close to the animals' teeth. Dogs enjoy scratches under the ear or on the neck.

4. Do not scream and run frantically around animals. If you are afraid, simply avoid eye contact, turning away from the animal and walking away as calmly as possible. Children, for their own safety, must be taught to behave calmly and gently.

In my mind, while I understand the concept of human–dog conflict, I don't believe it needs to be a *conflict*. We can learn how to co-exist and help each other. We have done this for millennia. It does not have to be 'us' versus 'them'. Dogs are designed to fit perfectly well in our society and find a way to make themselves useful to us. All we need to do is understand them better.

Lessons Learnt

During the course of the project, I learnt a lot. Of these, the first thing that jumped out at me was that while streeties did end up in conflicts with humans on rare occasions, there was a conspicuous absence of the so-called 'behaviour problems' that are seen in pet dogs. Interestingly, these problems did surface in these dogs within weeks, if not days, of getting adopted and moving into homes. Did it have to do with the lifestyle of street dogs as opposed to that of our pet dogs, given the distinct difference in lifestyles? I found that the streeties engaged in physical activity are far less frenzied and more deliberate. However, when it came to mental activity, while our dogs were being asked to perfect repetitive obedience, streeties were perfecting meaningful survival skills, exploring new territories, building and negotiating complex social structures.

Consider the skill of crossing streets. This is no easy task. Let me illustrate this point with a story of a few friends who were visiting me from outside India. One day, they asked me where they could buy some silk, and I pointed at a shop just across the road from us. I watched them as they left. They hailed a taxi, which confused me. When they returned, they explained to me that they did not really know how to cross the street, so they decided to take a cab to take a U-turn and reach the other side. Bangalore traffic is challenging, even for me, yet I see street dogs cross these streets with ease. I have seen a few do it on their own and a few others with help. They look around to see if any human is ready to cross the street and then inconspicuously join them. One needs to really witness this to see how smart they are. I can't help but ask myself if the puzzles, games, activities and training we design for our pet dogs are sufficient to engage their minds. It reminds me of a quote from one of my favourite books, *The Hitchhiker's Guide to the Galaxy*. Marvin, the paranoid android, often repeats:

> *'Here I am, brain the size of a planet,*
> *and they tell me to take you up to the bridge.*
> *Call that job satisfaction?'*

During my study, I have come to respect streeties for not just what they are capable of, but for all that they do for us. Many people who feed dogs will tell you that the dogs will diligently raise an alarm about shady characters who might be lurking around their neighbourhoods. The first few nights I tried to film the dogs, they woke up the entire neighbourhood. In one of the neighbourhoods I was doing my study, the people had built a particularly good bond with the streeties. Children played on the streets, and the adults seemed comfortable to leave the children in the care of these dogs if they had to step away for a few minutes. I have seen that once streeties befriend our dogs, they guard our dogs from other belligerent ones. We know they keep rat populations in check. There's a lot they do for us, but before ending this section, I must throw in this one last anecdote to illustrate how valuable they can be to us.

Bangalore is not the safest of cities for women: some women carry pepper spray for protection and some enrol in

self-defence classes. I count on the streeties instead. The first
thing I do when I find myself standing on quiet roads, late
at night, waiting for my cab to arrive, is to look around for
friendly street dogs, call them over and start petting them.
I keep them close until my cab arrives. Dogs hate conflict,
and if something were to happen, I know that they will at
least raise hell and draw attention. Studies show us that dogs
can and do differentiate between trustworthy people and
suspicious people. Simply put, they do take sides, and I have
no doubt in my mind that after petting a dog for ten seconds,
a streety will take mine. Dogs are ultimate team members,
and it's so useful to have them on your team, especially in
situations like this. The more I learn about them, the more
I come to realize that I can count on these animals. When
we don't understand them, we dismiss them as a nuisance,
but they are wired to be useful to us. When we understand
that, they become assets. So why not put a little effort into
understanding these fascinating animals and learning how
to coexist? They seem ready to do it and are willing to make
themselves useful. Why would we turn down their offer?

LIVES OF STREETIES: THE QUANTITATIVE STUDY

This final essay is a presentation of the actual findings
of the quantitative part of the 'Lives of Streeties' project.
For this study, each day, I picked an hour of the day,
marked out the standard route to walk on and recorded
the activity snapshot of all dogs I observed along this

route. I repeated this for every hour of the day. I averaged my recordings, and this is what I found.

Sleeping and sleeping-curled-up are, by far, the most frequent activities. Resting, foraging and standing are the next most prominent activities. Walking and trotting come next. Of course, there are a host of other activities that can be observed in much lower frequency: barking, grooming, begging, stretching, scratching, playing, pooping, peeing, rolling, and getting petted by people. I grouped these activities and compared them to see if we can gain more insights. The first comparison I did was between how many dogs were awake versus how many were asleep. The breakup looks like this:

- Asleep: 40 per cent
- Awake: 60 per cent

Awake versus Asleep

■ Asleep (40%) ■ Awake (60%)

This is very interesting, because you must remember that sleeping is just one activity among everything that streeties do in the day and accounts for more than a third of all activities. Sleeping is most likely under-represented in this study, because a lot of their sleeping happens during the day, when they are mainly hidden in drains and in homes, perhaps to escape the heat or the traffic. This explains why the total number of dogs observed during the hot afternoon hours of the day were much lower than average.

The next question on my mind was what the dogs were doing when awake. To visualize this, I regrouped the entire data into those on their feet and those not on their feet. An interesting picture emerges:

- Not on their feet: 59 per cent
- On their feet: 41 per cent

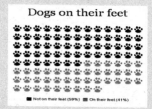

This seems to suggest that, even when awake, streeties don't seem to be very active. Close to 60 per cent of this graph is represented by dogs sleeping, sitting, lazing, basking in the sun or in the cool night wind, enjoying the act of watching life go by. This left me with the final question of how much these dogs move. I regrouped the entire data into two fresh buckets—dogs that moved and dogs that did not move. It turns out many of the dogs that were on their feet were just standing.

- Not moving: 77 per cent
- Moving: 23 per cent

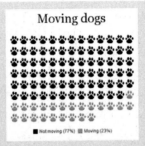

Moving dogs

■ Not moving (77%) ■ Moving (23%)

Less than a quarter of these observations included dogs moving. 'Moving' included activities such as walking, trotting, running, pooping, peeing, playing and foraging. For those of us who have paid attention to what free-ranging dogs do, this does not come as a surprise at all. We have seen dogs spend most of their time being rather lazy. This does seem to be consistent with behaviours of most predators in nature, who are rarely frenzied and are mostly lazing. Not surprisingly, another independent study in Kolkata by a team of behaviour scientists reveals very similar numbers.

I have been asked whether street dogs sleep so much to conserve energy for hunting or because they lead very stressed lives. However, neither of the above can be valid explanations. As I mentioned earlier, these dogs are rarely seen hunting and seem to be preferential scavengers and beggars. Most of them seem to be very relaxed in their movements, with far too few running or showing any frenzied movements. Most movement seems to be relaxed walking, interspersed with short distances of light trotting. Streeties are very nimble dogs, and their movement seems so effortless that I find it hard to imagine that they need to conserve much energy. In fact, our Labradors and Pugs seem to expend far more energy in regular movement around our home. It is also unlikely that they lead stressed lives—certainly not the dogs I studied. Most of the dogs in my study lived in neighbourhoods that were largely tolerant and provided adequately for dogs. Most dogs did not seem to be wary and seemed quite relaxed. They did not display any behaviour typically associated with stress, so I have no reason to believe they were so.

My study area did marginally touch upon what might have been a more stressful environment—the main road and a little slum nearby. Dogs here were a bit resource-starved, and it is likely that they rested less due to the busy streets. My observations showed that they also seemed more active, but this version of the study did not capture data on that.

I am inclined to believe that left unto themselves, *dogs choose to not be very active.* They seem to need far less movement than I had imagined. When we think of street dogs, we conjure up images of them leading highly active lives involving lots of car-chasing, playing, fighting and strutting around. Contrary to this commonly held belief, the streeties in my study seemed to prefer one activity over all else—sleeping.

CHAPTER 7

RESPECTING THE MIND

The Garden and Bungalow

Once I got back from Norway in late 2013, the first thing I had to do was to find a place to practise. I posted on my social media that I need help to run a dog behaviour consultancy. A pet parent got in touch with me and had an interesting offer. He had rented a bungalow and set up an office inside the bungalow for his team, but the bungalow was inside a piece of property with a huge garden which was not really being used. He was willing to let me use it for a very reasonable rent. I visited the building and my heart jumped up to my mouth. The location was brilliant. It was in the heart of the nicest part of Koramangala, and the building was a gorgeous, huge Bangalore bungalow. The garden had a lot of potential, and there was a lot dogs could do in it. I took no time to finalize the deal. Having shook on it, I stood in front of the place and tried to imagine what this place would be like, while I waited for Uttam to arrive. He arrived carrying a small gift for me. I unwrapped the box and found a lock inside it. He smiled and said to me, 'Congratulations, you are now a small business owner.' I proudly put the padlock on the door that led to the backyard and walked out with my head full of ideas on what I could do in this place. These were fun times, and I was beginning to discover the joys of my current profession.

Discovering Turid's Way

The bungalow will always be special to me because that is where I finally learnt leash-walking. My first attempt at trying to do loose-leash walking in India came from a place of fear and extreme lack of confidence. Given how busy Indian roads are, I attempted loose-leash walking on a short leash. It did not work, just as Turid had warned. With the bungalow being located on a very calm street, I now had the confidence to try this out with a long leash. Voila! Things started falling into place.

The bungalow was very close to where we lived then, and we would often try to bring our dogs to this peaceful street to walk on. However, we had to cross one busy street to get there, which posed the biggest challenge. It was the street where Nishi would lunge at other dogs, and it was on that street that I had fallen flat on my face trying to hold her back. It was on that street that she would often bolt because of traffic exhaust misfires or large trucks hurtling down. Since our walks would start on this note, it was hard to calm down for the rest of the walk. We'd have great walks on some days and terrible walks on other days. That cursed street was causing me to pull, teaching Nishi to pull in return. These walks were stressing us out so much that Uttam and my marriage started to suffer. My anxiety was escalating rapidly. All for a leash walk.

The wedge that the street was driving into our marriage went all the way through and split us apart two years later, in 2015. The separation did impact our dogs, and this book would not be complete if I did not talk about it. However, the separation also did something interesting to my understanding of loose-leash walks. When my husband and I separated, our dogs were left behind with my husband, based on our mutual decision. However, he was struggling to walk the two of them, especially past that one street. He figured out the simplest solution to the problem. He just decided to put the dogs in the car, drive past that dreaded street and, presto! he was in front of the bungalow, and had the most comfortable walks he could possibly have. On days when he could not do this, he would take the dogs out to poop and pee, bring them back and then just let them explore the parking lot. The parking lot is full of cars, and cars in India are always peed on by some dog or the other. They provide a wealth of sensory input for dogs, who are creatures of their nose. The dogs were perfectly fine spending some evenings just sniffing one car tyre after another, and returned home quite exhausted. Their overall bolting and pulling had reduced to a point where Uttam was now walking both girls comfortably on long leashes.

It is ironic how we needed that separation to figure out such a simple, workable solution to this problem. I spent several introspective hours trying to understand why I hadn't arrived at the solution myself. Eventually, I realized that I hadn't arrived at the solution because I had not given myself permission to make things easy for myself. I had believed that, as a professional, I had to know how to handle these difficult situations. Consequently, I was not willing to take it easy on my dog either. I also believed that they too had to be adept and suave at dealing with all situations.

It was a little before our separation that my anxiety was also beginning to peak. Later, during my introspective phase, I realized that to deal with my anxiety, I was beginning to alter my lifestyle to avoid sensory overloads. I had started using apps that delivered things home. I was using cabs to avoid driving. I worked from home when possible. I used calls and video conferencing in place of in-person meetings. When I discussed this with friends, I realized I am not alone and that there are several others who find it very hard to cope with the increasing stress levels of navigating a busy city like Bangalore. People are constantly looking for ways to escape the stress of city life. If a walk on Bangalore streets was that stressful for me, I can only imagine how much more stressful it would be for my dogs, who have a lesser understanding of the manmade world around us. They perceive the world from three to four feet below our eye level and have much sharper senses that hear, see and smell a lot more. Once I looked at it that way, it became easy for me to understand that I did not really have to push my dogs into having to deal with the stresses that I was struggling to deal with myself.

I had been trying to deal with this whole leash-walking thing by trying to repeatedly expose my dogs to stressors, in the hope that they would eventually learn to cope. However, my husband's approach of exposing my dogs lesser and lesser to what they found stressful taught me important lessons. The lesser I exposed them to stressors, the calmer my dogs seemed to get. The calmer they got, the easier it became for them to manage themselves in rare stressful situations and for me too to handle these situations. Of course, much earlier in the book, I put in an essay on how stress can alter learning. Obviously, the converse is true too: the calmer the individual, the more easily rational learning happens. When dogs lunge at other dogs or people, it's not because of lack of training but lack of social skills or some other unexplained stressor. If the stressors are removed, dogs are perfectly capable of learning social skills on their own from their peers. It's what dogs do!

While I am presenting this part of the story rather late in the book, you must remember that returning from Norway was early in my career. Getting the bungalow was still in the early days and discovering loose-leash walks outside this bungalow was nothing short of fascinating. Most importantly, it really was my first true experience of learning to live the Turid way.

Gaston

The new career was incredibly gratifying, but it was also challenging. These were brand-new ideas. None of my mentors were in the country to guide me. I was bound to make some big mistakes, which inevitably happened with lovely little Gaston. I will never forget Gaston! He pushed me to the next part of my journey.

I was invited to work with Gaston in 2014 when he bit his human. His biting had commenced rather suddenly and had escalated sharply. Sudden escalation of behaviours like this is typically an indication of an underlying health problem that has taken a sharp turn for the worse. I started the process of elimination, trying to figure out what might be wrong with Gaston, but before I had a chance to get to the bottom of it, Gaston was sent off to a board-and-train facility. Shortly after, he died there! I was consumed with guilt for not having got to the bottom of his medical issues fast enough. Gaston needed medical attention, not harsh training, but I did not have enough evidence to convince his humans of this. I felt that if I had been able to confidently point his parents in the direction of the right medical tests to talk to his vet about, he would have received the medical help he needed and still be alive.

I grieved for several days and eventually, upon Uttam's insistence, I gave Turid a call. I was expecting comforting kind words; instead, Turid in her inimitable fashion gave me brutal honesty. 'You don't know enough,' she said. Though I knew this in my heart, I protested to this idea by asking her if I, who was not a vet, was required to know symptoms of all diseases. Turid's reply was quite prompt. 'Yes, you need to know symptoms of diseases that present themselves as behavioural problems and behavioural manifestations of diseases.' She was categorical. As much as I hated what she was saying, I knew that she was right, and I knew that I just did not know enough.

A few months later, I received an email from Turid telling me she was commencing an educational programme in the US. Unlike her education in Europe, which consisted of fifteen modules—with each module lasting two days—spread over fifteen months, the education in the US consisted of seven modules, with each module lasting twice as long as the European ones. This meant less travel and, therefore, was slightly more practical for me. It still meant seven trips and all the additional expenditure involved, including stay, fees, food and any local travel. It seemed unreasonable and unaffordable, but after what happened to Gaston, I knew that I had to figure out some way to make it happen.

Uttam had started pushing me towards the course more and more, as he knew how important this education was to me. 'How am I going to make this happen, Uttam? It is highly unaffordable,' I complained. 'Something will work itself out,' he kept insisting. Sure enough, the first sign of something working out was Grace, the lady who was hosting Turid in the US, letting me know that she had an extra room in her house and that I could stay there for free for as long as I wanted. The next sign came when another classmate of mine,

Liz, offered scholarships for the most deserving and needy, and I got a big discount on my fees. At that point, I knew that I had to go ahead and take the plunge. I signed up for the class and bought the first set of tickets. I had just enough money for one more trip, and I was not really sure what I would do for the remaining five, but at this point, I was not in a place to let myself be paralysed by the fear of the unknown.

My Mind and Dogs

By the time I started my education in the US, my depression had been brewing for a while. It had started rearing its ugly head somewhere towards the latter part of my corporate life in mid-2009 and had been progressively getting worse every year. Nishi's horrendous accident had further exacerbated it, and my anxiety had started mounting. A year into Nishi's surgeries, my finances were drying up, and I had committed myself to a huge expenditure in terms of this education in the US. My work was suffering, and my confidence had taken a beating. Meanwhile, lady luck decided to stop being nice to my new career, and in 2014, I lost my garden in the bungalow. Uttam, too, had been out of a job for a while, and we had probably been in each other's face a little too much. All this tension made things incredibly difficult between the two of us. Our relationship was straining under all the pressure.

My education with Turid could perhaps not have happened at a more difficult time in my life. It involved travelling back and forth between India and the US several times that year. When I went to the US for the second time,

I had spent the last of the money in my bank. I had started questioning my decisions that had led me to this point. I started getting desperate, and I was not thinking straight. I wanted to get myself some coffee and considered going to the department store, hoping to be able to afford at least the smallest pack of coffee and sugar, until I realized that I was in the US. The smallest pack I could find seemed to be large enough to feed me and an entire village. I just moaned, trying to suppress my anger and frustration, not realizing that I could have bought myself the coffee and sugar and made it last the rest of the year, since I was going to be returning anyway. But that is precisely what depression and anxiety do—impede your ability to think straight and alter the way you think. This condition is called learnt helplessness and can impact both humans and animals alike.

Under the influence of the escalating depression, all my anxieties—including my social anxieties and travel anxieties—which were, in the past, merely just mild inconveniences, were now taking on a new avatar and becoming debilitating. While this felt terrible and something I would not wish on my worst enemy, it did give me a unique perspective into understanding dogs. I feel that my anxiety gave me a unique perspective on the way dogs experience life. It was the beginning of a new way of viewing this whole thing and a new way of making meaning of my internal struggles.

Food Aggression

The altered thinking patterns coupled with the depression and my now-diminished bank balance led me to believe that I had reached a point where I could not feed myself anymore. That was the lowest point in my life, and if I have come away with one thing from then, it is this: there really isn't any anxiety bigger than the that of not being able to feed oneself. Insecurity around food is absolutely the most terrifying thing one can experience. Having gone through it, I can now understand why an animal who experiences insecurity around food can snap. I also understand that when one feels insecurity of that kind, the only humane thing to do is to provide reassurance and comfort that one never has to face something that terrifying again.

Providing reassurance to a dog regarding food is not a very tall order. One way is to feed the dog in a safe and secure corner, where there are not too many people walking close to the dog as they eat, thereby giving the dog some privacy. If there are multiple dogs, it definitely helps to separate them, so that no dog ever feels like they might lose their food to another dog or must defend their food from others. It might also help dogs that have food insecurity to feed them several times a day and with food that is satiating and makes them feel very content at the end of the meal.

Unfortunately for me, it is not as easy for humans. I was unable to think of ways to earn enough money to continue my education and feed myself when in the US. Back home, I had lost the bungalow, but I had started consulting through home visits, and some income started trickling in. A bit later, I partnered with someone else from the industry and managed to afford a centre in Koramangala. Business started picking up, but it was not enough money for my visits to the US, so I started doing some odd jobs. During one of my trips to the US, I did some work in the garden for Grace, clearing weeds. I will never forget that day because it was hot as hell, I was starving and I needed what she was paying to buy food. Grace had seven dogs, and as I was weeding, one of her dogs' runny poop was in the weeds and it came flying into my face and my mouth. I just broke down crying, wondering how I had landed myself in this predicament, after having graduated as an engineer.

There were days I could think of no way to earn money. But American food portion sizes are massive and I had seen Americans throw away perfectly good food in intact packaging. Some days, I was so hungry and broke that I would go dig in dustbins for food. If I was in any better state of mind, I am sure I would have found better ways to make ends meet. Alas, this is what learnt helplessness looks like.

Bozo

By the end of my second module in the US, I was financially broke, emotionally broke and shortly thereafter, my marriage broke too. Uttam and I separated. We were aware that our separation would be very hard on the girls, and we had to be wise about their living arrangement. After careful deliberation, we both decided that it was best for the dogs if they stayed back with Uttam, because I had a lot more travel ahead of me and they needed stability. I was also unsure of my own emotional stability, and we both agreed that the girls needed to be shielded from that till I had a better handle on my mental health. With a heavy heart I agreed to leave them behind. Little did I know the toll it would take on me and the journey that lay ahead of me. But through the toughest of times, dogs continued to be my anchor.

In my deepest hour of need, Bozo saved me. Bozo is a special needs dog. He is a Rottweiler mix who suffers from a unique chronic condition called Exocrine Pancreatic Insufficiency or EPI, which causes him an incredible amount of discomfort and keeps him hungry all the time. His extreme condition drove him to unpleasant behaviours, including nipping. Not too many people are open to having a nipping Rottweiler. He was, therefore, abandoned several times before he landed in the house of a very generous person called Suman. Bozo's special needs brought me in touch with Suman a few months before my separation.

When I first met her, I explained to her why Bozo's biting needed us to look deeper into what was going on with his health. I also explained how some of the activities that she was doing with him were exciting him and consequently further agitating him to a point where he was so wired up that he was nipping everyone. The concept that I was explaining to her had seemed very unusual to many people in the past, and I met with a lot of resistance. So, the first time I tried to explain it to her, I was very cautious and hesitant, and slowly easing into the explanation. But Suman instantly saw reason in it and seemed to have an 'aha!' moment. 'Of course, all of this makes sense,' she said, 'I know this about human beings.' Suman was a bit of an expert on depression and anxiety in humans, and the idea of adrenaline overload made complete sense to her. That was the beginning of our friendship.

Eventually, when it was time for me to part ways with Uttam, Suman was there for me. She opened her doors to me and gave me the love and support I clearly needed. Bozo pitched in with timely licks and kisses and grounded me. Through my separation, there was always a dog that helped me hold on to my sanity and made it bearable.

Loneliness

The separation from my family lasted two painful years. I am going to spare you the details, but towards the end of 2016, Uttam and I decided to give our marriage another shot. This time, we got it right, but it was not a smooth transition and fairy-tale ending. In theory, it should have been. In these two years, I had gotten myself a new education, found a wonderful new place to work at, started teaching and found a fabulous batch of students. Moving in with my family should have made it all fall into place, but it did not. I was doing more and more of what I was good at and spending more time doing things that had earlier brought me joy—yet I felt no joy. I went back to my therapist, not able to understand why I was struggling when I really had no reason to struggle.

'Anhedonia,' she explained, 'is a classical problem with depression.' Anhedonia is the inability to feel joy. Depression changes the way the brain functions, and when the brain is functioning in an altered manner for a long time, it forgets some of its normal functions, including the ability to feel joy. Anhedonia is an important concept to understand because dogs experience it too. The brain chemistry is mostly the same. Dogs with anhedonia find it difficult to experience joy, which means that using treats to work with these dogs is usually pointless. In my next essay, I go into more detail on training and learning. But first, let's move past the despairing part of my story and on to better days.

It Didn't Kill Me

I am quite familiar with the adage that what does not kill you only makes you stronger. For people with depression, this is particularly meaningful. Today, I know that I am stronger. I am back with Uttam and my dogs. And my journey has made me develop an 'outside-in' perspective of my mental health. This has helped me understand my relationships with my dogs, my husband, my friends and me. It has forced me to recognize the impact this phase has had on all of them. It was a particularly hard pill for me to swallow when I realized that my depression and anxiety had a severe impact on Cheerwal. After her rescue, while we had done a lot to get her out of her shell, she had continued to remain skittish. However, the two years of my being away from them had really made her blossom and brought out her confidence. This was a ruthless reminder of how my turbulent mental health had impacted my own dog so negatively.

While the year I studied with Turid has been the hardest year of my life thus far, it showed me how tough I could really be. It taught me a lot and also built up my confidence. It showed me how amazing people really can be. It showed me how wonderful dogs are. Most importantly, it gave me an insight into how the mind works. I was able to relate to dogs in a way I never had before. It helped me develop empathy. I learnt to take a step back from observed behaviours and ask myself what was going on. While I had started out wanting to train dogs, I could now see that an animal's mind is far more complex and that I wanted to know how to unlock the potential of a dog's mind. I had learnt a new way of working with dogs. I was no longer a dog *trainer*.

LEARNING, TRAINING AND PUNISHMENTS

The study of knowledge—what is innate and what is learnt (and how we learn it)—is one of much interest to scientists, in the context of both humans and animals. We understand very little of what innate knowledge is and how it is transferred, and we recognize a few different ways in which learning happens, including through experimentation, observation and imitation, and external conditioning. Animals, too, are known to have these different ways in which they come to acquire knowledge that leads to observable behaviours. Understanding this matters.

An interesting thing to observe in this context is that there is a distinct difference between our pet animals and free-ranging animals. Free-ranging animals rely on a wide range of learning techniques, including experimentation and observation, but our pet animals are so heavily influenced by us that their learning may be dominated by our conditioning. This, in turn, may result in our inability to recognize what animals can learn without our influence.

The truth, however, is that our animals are capable of learning a lot, even without our input. For example, I have a fantastic video of Cheeru in communication with another dog called Blacky. Cheeru and Blacky did not really get along with each other, but for some reason, this particular time, they both decided to try to sort out their differences. We managed to capture the whole 2.44-minute interaction on camera. In this footage, the dogs exchange upwards of thirty instances of calming signals. Cheeru is a somewhat reactive dog, so this surprised me. It also made me realize that there is no way I could have taught her that entire sequence or even known what was required as part of that sequence. I am not sure how she came to learn all this or how much of it was innate, but none of it came from me.

Another example is of Nishi having gotten over her fear of dogs after her accident. She not only learned to cope with it, but also learnt to communicate so well with dogs that I often use her videos in my talks and classes to demonstrate how good she is at social protocols. None of it was my teaching. In fact, when she is around dogs, most times, I loosen the leash and step away and maintain pin-drop silence so that I do not end up influencing the interaction. The more I factor myself out of the situation, the better she seems to handle it.

Our observations show that different dogs prefer different signals. For example, lighter dogs may choose to use more of blinking, while darker dogs may choose to use more of licking of the lips. Cheeru is a very nimble dog, so she can be seen using more subtle signals such as blinking, licking of the lips, picking up her paw and subtle curves. Nishi is a big dog, a bit physically uncoordinated due to her health and partial blindness. She seems to prefer 'bigger' signals like pronounced curves, freezing or head turns. It seems that the dogs not only have an awareness on what signals to use but can also learn to fine-tune their communication based on how well it carries their message. I am certainly not involved in this part of their learning.

The last example I offer here is that of the superior problem-solving skills of streeties. These dogs, of course, are not under our care and are not as much influenced by what we wilfully teach them. Nevertheless, they seem to learn how to find people who can give them food, how to extract food out of containers, how to cross busy Indian streets, how to resolve conflicts with dogs and other animals, how to detect dangerous people and so much more. Their cognitive skills have not been studied, but for those of us who pay attention, it is remarkable, to say the least.

When we look at the examples above, it is not always evident how much of what they know and do is innate and how much of it is learnt or how they learn it. However, if we were to rely on our limited understanding of canine cognition and communication, we may not be teaching them the right lessons. For example, we know sitting to be a calming signal, but we do not know exactly how dogs use it, when they use it and what it is meant to communicate in different contexts. The calming signal observations we practise in class show us that there is far more nuance to these signals than we fully understand. Therefore, making them sit when the context calls for something else may result in a communication breakdown.

Then there are 'problem behaviours' that we see the need to change, because of the inconvenience it causes us. One way to achieve this is to punish the dog for engaging in them. Elizabeth Gershoff, an assistant professor at the University of Austin, Texas, has been studying punishment in the context of humans. The following are some of her findings that are also relevant in the context of dogs:

1. There is no study that has found a positive consequence when it comes to punishment. While it may stop a certain behaviour, it does not mean that the child learnt anything about why they were being punished or what was expected of them instead.

2. Punishments create something called 'hostile attribution bias' in the child, which causes them to expect people to be mean towards them and

for the world to be hostile. This, in turn, makes the child feel on edge and turn hostile themselves.

3. Studies of children across various cultures and ethnicities have proven that corporal punishment does real and measurable damage to their brains.

Another way to alter an animals' behaviour is with rewards, but the animal may be showing the behaviour as a way of expressing an internal state. Not getting to the bottom of what is causing it may leave the underlying issue unaddressed. The behaviour may also simply be part of a dog's normal ethogram. An ethogram is collection of behaviours that is considered normal for free-ranging members of a species, in their natural habitat. Simply put, this is just normal behaviour, and while it may seem inconvenient to us, not allowing the dog to engage in these behaviours may have dire consequences on the mental well-being of the animal. I have a few examples to help me discuss this idea.

1. Dogs may express fear through distance-creating signals such as lunging, snarling, growling or trying to run away. Several skilled professionals may be able to extinguish these behaviours, but the catch is that there really is no evidence that changing the behaviour can change the underlying emotion. Furthermore, in some cases, this fearful emotion may be coming from hidden physical discomfort. A dog may be nervous that

certain interactions could trigger pain, so the behaviours we see may be defensive reactions. However, if we just change the behaviour, then we do not know if the internal state changed. In my work, behaviours are like a meter that indicates the internal state of the dog, and altering the behaviour is like rigging the meter, depriving us of valuable information.

2. Consider the behaviours of destruction or chewing of objects. This is, in fact, part of a dog's ethogram. Sometimes, dogs may chew excessively, which could be an indication of something else going wrong. One reason could be that the animal is stressed, and chewing helps it ease this stress. Another could be a dog using the sensory input from the mouth for better sensory integration in uncertain situations. There also seems to be a correlation between ulcers and oral stereotypies. When I encounter this behaviour, the first thing I do is to try to meet the needs of the dog in as healthy a way as possible. In the meantime, I also launch an investigation to get to the bottom of what may be causing excessive chewing.

3. Consider the example of dogs wanting to sleep on our beds or sofas. This may not always work for us, but what can we observe of normal sleeping behaviours of dogs? Sleeping on elevated surfaces, sleeping in bursts and moving between

these bursts seems to be part of their ethogram. Dogs may prefer elevation to keep a lookout, a behaviour they do not need in our homes but is simply one they carry as part of their ethogram. I only speculate here on what may be resulting in it, but what we do know is that organisms need to feel comfortable in where and how they sleep. If that does not happen, it can compromise the quality of sleep, which in turn impacts behaviour. Therefore, instead of locking dogs in crates, giving them very limited options, could we instead consider taking away access just to the sofa or the bed we consider off limits, but still leave them with sufficient options that can cater to their preferences?

Dogs have many behaviours that we may not always understand and many ways of learning things too. Yet, the lives of our dogs are heavily controlled by us in terms of access to almost all the resources necessary for survival and welfare, such as food, water, social contact, sleep and movement. It is easy to end up being the primary driver of their behaviours, and therefore, it is imperative to be mindful of what we are asking of them. Should we be modifying their behaviours or trying to alter the internal state that drives a certain behaviour? Are some behaviours serving important functions in the dog? Should we even consider extinguishing those or just finding ways of engaging with them in other ways? Should we be aiming to teach them everything they know, or can we give them access to environments and other members of their species from whom they can learn? Should we give them opportunities where they can engage in some amount of safe trials and errors, and give them the pleasure of figuring out some meaningful life-lessons on their own?

CHAPTER 8

BEYOND BEHAVIOUR

Julia

I met Julia in the US in 2015. Julia Robertson is the pioneer of pioneer of Galen canine myotherapy. Turid had invited her over to conduct a four-day workshop for us. Julia combined a thorough knowledge of dog musculature, a keen eye for dog movement and an uncanny skill at understanding dog communication. This gave us another strong tool in our belt to help our dogs.

During Julia's workshop, we spent a lot of time watching animals' movement and posture, trying to see if they could provide clues as to the animals' wellness. For example, if an animal had pain in one of the joints in their legs, how would they hold it when they stood? Would they avoid putting weight on that leg, and if they did, how would that leg look when they stood? How would their movement look when they walked if their knee was causing the problem and they were trying to avoid bending the knee? Is there anything that we could learn from watching them sit or stand? If they are constantly favouring one side when sitting or lying down or when trying to get up, does that tell us something about the state of their limbs and muscles? These are the questions Julia had got us to start thinking about.

During one such exercise, we filmed two of the dogs walking up and down. Julia then worked on both these dogs, manipulating their muscles. This was a jaw-dropping moment for us. Both the dogs had shown intense resistance to touch and were quite reactive towards people trying to touch them. But here was Julia, massaging one dog after the other, with techniques that seemed to look fairly intense, and the dogs were willing to let her do it. As we watched in wonder, these dogs not only let her work on them but also went on to do something fascinating. They turned around after their treatment and came up to her and placed their head on her chest and stood there for a few seconds, making the entire class gasp.

These dogs came back the next day, and we filmed them walking again. What we saw then has stuck with me the most. Their gaits had changed! They were carrying their heads and necks better; they were looser at their limbs and flexing all their joints much better. They had a spring in their step. This was after *one* treatment. Julia called it 'myotherapy'. It felt like magic. Although I did not understand it, I knew I wanted this for Nishi.

The Storm after the Storm

As I said, Nishi's woes had not really ended with her accident. Just a little before her accident, we had noticed that she had a strange kicking motion in her hind legs. At first, we thought she was reacting to ants. Uttam and I would look at her paws but not find any ants. Realizing that there must be some other reason, we took her to the vet. At that time, the term patellar subluxation had been casually thrown at us. We didn't really think much of it then, and before we really had a chance to, the accident happened. The first few months after the accident went into repairing all the damages caused by it. By mid-2011, Nishi had already been to hell and back. Now, we were being told that we had to take this patellar subluxation thing more seriously.

The patella is the kneecap and sits in a groove on the leg bone, held in place by soft tissue, somewhat like being taped in place. If the groove is not deep enough, the kneecap is not sitting tightly enough and can slip out of position. When the patella slips out, it can be excruciatingly painful. I once saw it happen to my aunt. She was screaming in pain until it was pushed back into place. It does jump back easily, as if by spring action, and the pain seems to subside quickly.

Clearly, Nishi's kicking action was her trying to slip her patella back into position. We were not too concerned, because she did not seem too concerned. However, the frequency with which she was kicking started increasing. We were still not too concerned, because we felt that she was in pain just for a few seconds at a time, and we had been through enough to even contemplate another complication with a puppy that had barely completed her first birthday. We were informed again that the problem was not the pain. The problem was that the patella moving so much would slowly start grinding down her bones until the nerve endings became exposed. When that happened, she would be in constant unbearable pain, which would only worsen with age.

What did this puppy have in store? Whose sins was she paying for?

With a heavy heart, we prepared for another surgery. We learnt that the bones would be sculpted to make the kneecap fit better, and the spring mechanism would be tightened and repositioned so that it would hold the kneecap firmly in position. We consoled ourselves that the procedure sounded simple enough. After an encounter where we were nervous about having potentially left behind a part of her brain on the road, this sounded relatively simple.

After the surgery, we decided to stay home for several days and take care of Nishi until she recovered. We took her to physiotherapy every day, dressed her, iced her and administered hot packs. She suffered through all of it without complaining. A few days later, we took her back for a check-up and the vet almost burst into tears. It turned out that the patella had slipped out again and healed there. It was now stuck completely out of position. She was back under the knife again. And again. And again. She was in so much pain that there would be nights she would just sit up and stare into space for almost an hour—not moving, doing nothing. I would wake up and sit with her. I did not know what I could do to ease her pain, so I would just sit beside her and stare with her. Her leg was in a cast for so long that she lost all muscle mass in it. We could not take her on walks because the walk could put pressure on the kneecap, but she needed the exercise to build her muscles. The situation was going from bad to worse, so on the next scheduled surgery date, we decided to take a step back and ask more questions. Questions we should have perhaps asked earlier, if only we had known better. We learnt that this surgery was a complicated one with a very small success rate, getting smaller with each failed attempt. At this point, we decided to put a stop to all surgeries.

Nishi's condition, however, was degenerative; it would get worse with age and the surgeries had failed to rectify it. Where were we to go from here? We held each other and cried. Where had we gone wrong? Would our puppy, one with boundless energy, lose her leg? Were her best days already behind her, with every day bringing new pain? We had started spiralling down a bottomless pit of darkness and despair. But there was a little voice inside our heads urging us to hold on to hope. If Nishi could speak out, her voice would perhaps sound like that. It told us, 'Do you see how Nishi has put blind faith in you and followed you down every path you have asked her to take? She has faith in you. Why do you not have that faith?' We picked ourselves up, dusted ourselves off and got to work.

First, we had to address the loss of muscle tone in her leg. If muscle tone had to be brought back, the muscles needed to move. However, she would not land that leg; it was far too painful. So we could not really ask her to walk on it because we knew it would be adding load on her knees. Instead, we decided to try swimming. Short-snout dogs really do not like swimming, and there was no way we would stress her out more than she already was. So Uttam and I got into the pool and held her on our shoulders, nudging her to just paddle between us, a few inches at a time. Nishi is a brave dog, if nothing else. She is game to try anything, so she tried it out. Soon, she discovered that she knew how to handle the water, which seemed to give her joy and she gained confidence. Within a week, she started looking forward to her swimming sessions. We would take her swimming four to five times a week, for two and a half months, and it was a joy to watch each time. Within a few weeks, she was landing her leg; within the following few months, she was running on it!

However, we knew that the swimming had not permanently fixed her leg and that an underlying bone problem meant that we had only bought ourselves some time. As the bones moved over each other, with continued usage, they would wear out; eventually, this problem would resurface in her later years. Sure enough, by the time I had gone to meet Julia, Nishi's leg had started to show signs of struggle. She was slow to sit or get up; she would injure her leg frequently and limp often; and she had a funny seated posture that suggested that her knees had never fully recovered. I could see that this would all deteriorate quickly and was desperate to find her respite. When I saw what Julia was capable of, I knew that I had to figure out a way to get her to see Nishi.

Canine Myotherapy

'I want you to see something,' I told Julia, and turned around and pulled my shirt away from my shoulder, towards the back, to expose the tattoo of Nishi's face. 'That's adorable!' Julia exclaimed. 'That's Nishi. I need to figure out how to get you to meet her,' I told Julia. She nodded understandingly and said, 'Yes, sure, I understand. She has a problem in her hind legs, does she?'

My jaw dropped.

How did Julia know about Nishi's hind legs? Now that I know how Julia pieces it together, this is how she works it out.

It obviously starts with Nishi's right hind leg, where she has patellar subluxation. Because of this and the surgeries that she has had, that leg has far less strength than she needs on it. Therefore, she uses more and more of her left hind leg and her front legs. Over-utilization of the left hind leg resulted in that leg getting stiffer, and eventually, her left hind leg became far more vulnerable to injury. Nishi also uses her front legs a lot more to give her the drive to propel herself forward. When seated, her buttocks are usually on the floor and her hind legs stretched out. They are in no position to bend to give her the drive to get her butt off the ground. Instead, she rocks forward, shifting her weight on to her front legs and almost pulling herself up with her neck and shoulders. Thus, her front legs end up doing much more work than they were designed to, leading to those muscles getting bulkier and bigger.

In Julia's experience, when the neck muscles are compromised like this, it results in a very thick neck and dry nose. In the tattoo that I showed Julia, she observed Nishi's extremely dry nose and thick neck! That is how Julia had pulled a Sherlock! I can almost picture her saying, 'Elementary, my dear Sindhoor,' even if Sherlock never did!

That was my introduction to Canine Myotherapy.

Understanding My Injuries

After my introduction to Julia's skills, I knew I had to get her over to India. The universe seems to have conspired to make it happen, because in May 2017, Julia and a team of three other myotherapists found themselves enjoying mangoes and the monsoons in India. The agenda was to introduce the field to India and for me to complete on my own myotherapy diploma practicals. Julia's introduction to myotherapy practicals is one that will never leave me. The very first day was spent on assessing my muscles, my injuries and working on my muscles to help me understand what these techniques were and how they brought relief.

Julia asked me to stand up straight, and she took one long look at me. 'Is that really how you stand?' she asked.

'Yes. Why?'

'Did you know that one shoulder of yours is higher than the other?'

'Huh?'

'Go stand up against this wall. Can I make a mark on the wall with a pen?' Julia then made some marks on the wall and asked me to look.

The wall had tiles on them, which made it easy to compare the two ink marks that presented the height of both my shoulders. Sure enough, there was a centimetre-and-a-half difference between the two. She continued to examine me, watched me walk, and then asked me if I was experiencing any discomfort in my legs. I pointed at my left knee and said, 'That hurts.'

'Okay, let's examine the muscles around it, shall we?'

Julia palpated the muscles on my leg, around my knees. 'Well, I see that you have pain in your left knee, but you do have an injury in your right leg too, don't you?' I did. Julia palpated the muscles a little bit more and then said, 'Well, the injury on your right leg is actually older than the one on your left. Isn't it?' She was right about that too. I had sustained this injury during my dancing days, when I was preparing for my Rangapravesha. She continued to palpate the muscles and narrowed it down exactly to the muscle that I had injured back then. Finally, Julia proceeded to stitch up the story of my muscles.

It started out with me injuring my right inner thigh, because of which my right leg was unable to take enough load. So, without thinking about it, I had started shifting the load to my left leg. Nature has designed human legs to take 50 per cent of the load, so when one leg starts taking more than 50 per cent, it sustains stress, making it more susceptible to injury. So now, almost a decade after the initial injury, my left knee was responding to the pressure and I was experiencing pain in my left leg. Due to the imbalance in my knees, my utilization of my hip muscles, my lower back and my upper back are all impacted. At this point, not only do I suffer from pain in my knees but also stiffness and pain in my back, shoulders and neck.

All of this is very evident when one watches me move. The pain is evident, but the story seems evident only to Julia. This is what myotherapy is. Julia's skill, to be able to look at the posture and movement of a person as the story of the injuries is what makes her an expert in her field. With humans, this is not really a necessary skill because a human can point to their pain and tell their own story. I could have easily told her that I did sustain an injury many years ago on my right leg if she had asked me for my case history. I could have told her that to this day, I continue to experience pain from the old injury. A dog, on the other hand, is not only incapable of expressing all this, but will also actively try to hide signs of pain. It is for this reason that we need to know more about our dog's body and how it works. This following essay is a brief introduction to a dog's anatomy, distilling just the details that will help a pet parent understand how lifestyle can impact a dog's muscles and health.

THE FLOATING LIMB AND REST OF DOG ANATOMY

Let's take it from the top, as they say. In humans, the head sits on the neck supported by the collar bone or the clavicle. Dogs don't exactly have a collarbone. The neck is held away from and in front of the body. The head is a very heavy body part that is held up against gravity by several strong muscles connecting it to the ribcage, chest, back, shoulders and front legs. These muscles need to work quite hard to pick up the head against the gravitational pull of the earth. In their relaxed state, they keep the head in a neutral position. This is called the **natural head carriage** of a dog.

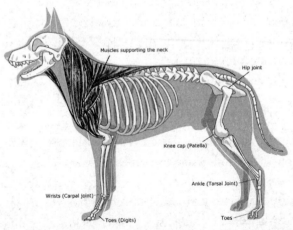

A brief guide to the important joints of the canine body and an overview of the muscles in the neck that support the head and shoulders and enable movement.

Note: This image only illustrates the muscle, not the natural head carriage of a dog. The natural head carriage is a lot lower.

However, dogs live in our world, where all the activity happens three feet above their head. They need to keep lifting their head to be involved. Living with humans also means a lot of interaction with humans, which requires eye contact, so pet dogs are inclined to lift their head a lot more than their free ranging counterparts. Collars and other products that go around the dog's neck also require them to pick up their head when walking. All these actions overwork the muscles on the back of the neck, leading them to remain shortened for extended periods of time. This, of course, causes discomfort. This is easy for someone like me to understand, who is of short stature and used to be a first-bencher in college. Back then, I would spend the entire day with my neck craned to look up at the professor, and by the end of the day, I would suffer from back and shoulder pain.

In dogs, the neck is also attached to the leg. If the neck is lifted, the muscles attaching the neck to the shoulders are stretched. This impacts movement, since the shoulders are involved. Let's take a closer look at the front leg to understand movement in dogs. The shoulder blades (scapula) in humans are attached to the arm bone (humerus) on one side and the collar bone (clavicle) on the other side. In a dog, since the clavicle is almost non-existent, where does the scapula connect? The answer is that it doesn't really connect to anything, making it a floating limb! The shoulder bone is merely placed on either side of the ribcage, tied with strong bands of muscles, and is expected to glide smoothly on the rib cage. The front limb trades in load-bearing functions in favour of flexibility. The drive and strength come from the rear legs, which have a very robust ball-and-socket joint at the hips. The front legs are designed to provide steerability, much like a car. Assuming the dog does not jump up and down as much, this arrangement works just fine. While streeties climb up on to tall surfaces, you can also often see them being very smart about charting out a low-impact path for climbing down. They rarely jump down and rarely on to smooth, hard surfaces. However, the lifestyles that our dogs are subjected to include a lot of jumping from cars, furniture, beds, in play or various other activities we engage our dogs in on very smooth, hard flooring.

Objects such as sofas, cars and beds were designed for optimal usage for human beings. When getting off a bed, we elegantly swing our legs off the bed, plant them softly on the ground and just rise. Dogs, on the other hand, are not exactly replicating this movement. All four of their limbs are on the bed, and when they get off, they are jumping off the bed or sofa clearing 15 to 20 inches each time. This would be the equivalent of us not actually getting up from a sofa or a bed but jumping off them each time. One can only imagine the impact this would have on our joints if we repeated this action frequently.

Now let's consider the case of dogs. A dog does not land on its hind legs, but on the front legs. The front legs do consist of the 'wrist' and 'elbow' joints in a dog, but the 'shoulder joint' is missing and instead, the leg is fastened to the body with muscles, which does give the front leg a bit more flexibility. But each time they jump, the muscle bands that attach the front limbs to the torso absorb this shock, and in the process, they get very rapidly stretched out. This kind of repeated rapid stretching can badly injure the muscles, increasing scar tissue and reducing the elasticity of the muscle over a period of time. Typically, such dogs end up with muscular damage between their shoulder blades, which can make them reluctant to move their front legs freely, reducing the range of movement and making it look like they're holding their elbows very close to their body.

Let's move from the front legs to the hind legs of a dog. These are meant to be the primary limbs that propel a dog, enabling them to move forward, get up and sit down. But due to poor breeding practices, many of our dogs are suffering from diseases that impact joints of the hind leg, including arthritis, hip dysplasia and patellar subluxation. The unfortunate truth about these diseases is that they are hard to diagnose early, not really curable and they get progressively worse with poor utilization of the joints. In such diseases, the joints are not perfectly aligned. Consequently, they do not move smoothly, resulting in friction, which further wears down the tissues at the point of contact, causing more damage and discomfort. As things get progressively worse for the dog, they try to protect those joints, be it at the hip or the knees, by reducing movement and thus, reducing the amount of power they can generate from these limbs. To compensate for the lack of power in the hind legs, the dogs may begin to use more of their front legs, to either push themselves up or to propel themselves forward. This might be noticeable in dogs in the form of an odd sway in the hips, stiffness in the hind legs, combined with telltale signs in the front with over-developed shoulder muscles, extremely thick neck muscles and a dry snout.

Finally, let us look at the feet of the dog. Dogs don't plant their whole feet on the floor. Observe their feet. You might notice a knob-like structure at the back of their feet, a few inches off the ground. That's approximately where their feet actually end. Essentially, dogs are walking on their toes. Animals which do so are known as digitigrade animals. Dogs are built this way to optimize for speed but this compromises on the amount of traction they get. Now, imagine the surfaces they are walking on. In Indian homes, most of the surfaces our dogs are walking on are smooth, marbled floors or vitrified tiles. To understand the impact of this kind of movement on these tiles, imagine walking on stilettos 24x7 and how little traction that can offer. These surfaces do not provide enough traction for such a small area touching the ground. It's not rare to notice dogs skid all over the place. This skidding is not to be ignored. It can cause sudden stretching of muscles, which causes muscle tears and injuries.

Unfortunately, with dogs, soft tissue injuries are very hard to catch—not only because these are not seen in typical diagnostic tests, but also because dogs are notorious for masking them and often don't even realize they have injured themselves during play, due to the pain-numbing effects of adrenaline. Hence, it is important to pay attention to the types of activities dogs engage in and the surfaces they walk on. Soft tissue injuries are easy to ignore, but do have long-term implications if ignored. Remember the story of the muscle I pulled during my dancing days and the impact it has on my left knee today. An injury sustained by a puppy may well result in arthritis in later years, and sadly, we may never see the connection. Thus, exercising caution may be our only viable option in this regard.

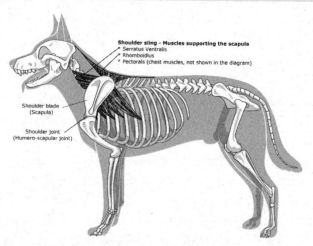

Shoulder sling - Muscles supporting the scapula
* Serratus Ventralis
* Rhomboidius
* Pectorals (chest muscles, not shown in the diagram)

Shoulder blade
(Scapula)

Shoulder joint
(Humero-scapular joint)

The front limb is not attached to the body via a joint. A few muscles act together to connect the front limb to the torso and enable movement. These muscles form a 'shoulder sling'.

Consent

It was very impressive for me to watch Julia talk about my injuries as if she was there through it all. What followed next was even more fascinating. I realized that the techniques that the myotherapists were using were similar to the ones used in sports massages. Having been through those, I know how painful they are. 'Wait a minute, how are you going to get a dog to sit through such a treatment and not bite you? Do you use muzzles and leashes?' I had seen pictures and videos of what they were doing, and I had not seen any leashes or muzzles, which began to scare me. I had worked with plenty of dogs with behavioural issues, and I knew that dogs in pain are very sensitive to touch. In fact, what had led me to Julia was my realization that most of the biting cases that had been brought to me were somehow related to pain. The thought of delivering treatment of this nature to some of those dogs was scary, to say the least. 'Nope, we don't use muzzles or leashes. In fact, we don't even use massage tables because then the dogs don't have the opportunity to walk away. We work on the floor, so that the dogs can walk away from us and come back to us when they feel that they need this treatment. Not only do we not have to restrain them, they actually tell us what needs to be done to them,' Julia told me.

I did not really understand what she was telling me, but I do now. Think about it this way: sometimes, when your back is hurting, you might push your palm against your back or push your back against a hard surface for pain relief. How many times do we rapidly rub our injury if we bump against something? This is good touch and pressure, the kind that relieves pain. Then there is bad pressure, the kind of pain that we pull away from. If you have a stiff shoulder or back, and someone pushes their thumb into it or even touches it lightly, it is annoying at best and painful at worst. The body does differentiate between these touches, guiding us on what to push into and what to pull away from. Julia demonstrated both to me, poking me in a way that hurt, and then in a way that, while somewhat painful, was not repulsive and was progressively making it better. I've come to realize now that animals are far better than us at listening to what their bodies are telling them and seem far more intuitive in this regard.

This is the point at which Julia's and Turid's ideas overlap. Both put a lot of faith in a dog's inherent ability to be highly intuitive and work on reading them better, instead of trying to get prescriptive about what is good for them. 'Give them a choice, and they take better decisions than you can ever imagine,' seems to be the consistent message.

Pain, not Sorrow

It's never easy to tell pet parents that their dogs may be experiencing discomfort or pain. It is very upsetting to imagine that they may be hiding their pain just so they can keep up with us. In one of my conversations with Julia, I broke down and cried, telling her how bad I felt for Nishi. Julia asked me to think about my own pain. Thanks to my dancing and running days, I have sustained my fair share of injuries, which have resulted in poor musculature and knee pain.

She pointed out that while I do have a lot of injuries and pain, I do not have a poor quality of life, nor am I a sad person. Yes, I do have good and bad days, and yes, there are some activities that I cannot engage in. Sometimes I wince in pain, but that does not mean I experience sorrow. It only means that I will try and avoid certain situations and I will limit the set of activities that I can do.

Similarly, with our dogs, their ailments do not necessarily mean that they are unhappy or uncomfortable all the time, but it does mean that they may benefit from avoiding a few things that can worsen their ailments. Therefore, as pet parents, we must equip ourselves with some knowledge. The rest of this chapter will aim to educate you on various aspects of a dog's health. We start with understanding pain.

DEEP DIVE ON PAIN

All of us are familiar with pain and discomfort. Unfortunately, many of us are also familiar with that one annoying person who will approach us when we are in throes of pain and, in a badly timed attempt to sound profound, will say something like, 'It's all in your head. Let it go.' Pain is strange. It seems highly subjective and personal. Two people who are subjected to the same pain-inducer might experience and react to it very differently. Some pain also seems to mask other pain. What seems painful until yesterday may seem irrelevant in the light of new and more intense pain. Was the old pain all in my head then? What about the new pain?

Is it also all in my head or is it real? Sometimes, it is possible to 'forget' pain, like old injuries, then suddenly 'remember' it: just thinking about an old injury could make it hurt again.

So what is pain?

The International Association for the Study of Pain (IASP) defines it as follows:

1. Pain is invisible.
2. Pain is a feeling.
3. Pain is unpleasant.
4. Pain feels like damage.

It seems that pain is indeed a manifestation of the brain, although, if you have ever had any serious injury, you perhaps would have felt that it was as real as the air you breathe or the soil that you walk on. Why is the brain concocting such a powerful and unpleasant feeling? The answer is *protection*. An injured muscle induces discomfort when you try to use it, so that you stop and give it time to heal and recover. If you ingest something your body does not accept, it could respond with allergies, nausea, cramps, etc. All these responses are associated with discomfort and pain. Eventually, what one vividly recollects is not the diagnosis but the discomfort. It's this that makes you avoid eating something inappropriate for your body the next time. This is how the body protects itself from injury.

Do other animals experience discomfort? There have been several studies that have attempted to answer this question. At this point, I am not going to wait for the results of the studies but assume that all animals do experience pain and discomfort. The risk of not doing so has led us to inflict some of the most barbaric, gut-wrenching, sustained pain on animals. Even the studies that attempt to answer the question of whether animals feel discomfort inflict unnecessary and unjustifiable pain on them. If we are to talk about the welfare of any animal, the conversation only begins after we acknowledge and agree that animals feel pain and discomfort, that it is unpleasant by definition and that pain is personal and subjective.

Perhaps a reason for people to not accept that animals feel pain is because they express it differently. Animals are often stoic about their discomfort. For an animal, there is no point whining about a broken leg. They cope with it, make necessary adjustments and just move on. A deer in a forest hurt by a tiger does not have the luxury to 'take the day off' or go to the doctor or even complain to his circle of friends. By the time an animal begins to scream, one can be sure things have gotten very bad. Often, the screaming is a sign that the animal is crying out for help or trying to deter further infliction of pain. Dogs are no exception. Consider my Nishi. The day when she was lying on that gurney with her face split open, there was not a peep from her. All the screaming was finished when she was first hit, until we pulled her out from under the car. By the time we had gotten her to the vet, she didn't scream at all. If she could stop expressing pain in a situation as extreme as that, it only shows me how much animals will tolerate before overtly expressing their discomfort. Just thinking about this makes my eyes well up. Yes, Nishi is a tough puppy, but she was not an exception. Most dogs are tough, and this often works against them in that it is easy for illnesses and diseases to go unnoticed. By the time we realize there is a problem, the animal might have been suffering for a long time.

The Health Behaviour Connect

After attending Julia's workshop for the first time in the US, I could not help but observe and analyse muscles and movements of dogs during my behaviour consults. Suddenly, I felt like I was observing odd musculature and movement in most dogs that were coming to me. I started wondering if I was getting it all wrong. I will never forget the day I had two Cocker Spaniel puppies turn up at my centre, both exhibiting similar behavioural problems and muscular issues. These two pet parents went ahead and got x-rays done. The x-rays revealed nothing, crushing my confidence, so I decided to stop looking at the pain angle.

However, there was a mounting pile of cases that looked very similar to each other. Most of them involved dogs with odd musculature and gait, coupled with unresolved behavioural issues. Eventually, six months later, both the Cocker Spaniels' parents got back to me, confirming to me that later x-rays had revealed the dogs had hip dysplasia. One of those puppies, Streak, continued to come to me as part of my case studies and helped me become a myotherapist. Streak had come to me because he had bitten a few times. If I were him, and I was in constant pain, I too would be very irritable and very likely to snap easily. When Streak first started experiencing discomfort, he was just a tiny puppy in a family that loved him to bits. I'm quite sure he was picked up quite frequently, and when he played with other dogs or people, it would have been easy to engage in rough-play and he is likely to have hurt himself repeatedly. Thus, it is understandable that Streak might, in general, be wary of any form of engagement that involves touch. And one day, that general wariness might, under some combination of circumstances, lead to snapping. We all snap, but when a dog snaps, it's a bite. It often means dire consequences for the dog as well as the person. Thankfully, in Streak's case, his loving family is working on getting him all the help he needs to feel relief, including making lifestyle changes that can at least slow down the degeneration of these joints.

The pain–aggression connection is relatively easy to understand. It is not that difficult to imagine that an animal in pain is likely to lash out. However, what is a little harder to understand is the pain–hyperactivity connection. Chronic pain is hard to recognize in dogs. Far too often, when I first mention to pet parents that their dogs might be in pain, I get a standard response that usually goes something like, 'No way, Sindhoor! It's not possible. You should see him run like the wind when we take him to the park.' Sadly, a dog that runs a lot does not imply a perfectly healthy dog.

Dogs, like most animals, need to hide their pain. Nature demands this of most animals. Dogs also love to keep up with their people. To do so and still cope with the pain, a dog's body starts generating adrenaline, which numbs pain. This is how dogs manage to keep up with their humans. However, the side effect to this excessive adrenaline is residual cortisol. Together, they can make dogs hyper. We've already discussed at length how this leads to behaviours such as excessive barking, inappropriate urination, jumping on people, destruction of objects, zoomies, lack of concentration, inability to learn rationally and other possible obsessive behaviours. Naturally, these dogs first end up at a behaviourist's doorstep. Therefore, it is critical that behaviourists be able to notice signs of physical discomfort and illness. It is truly shocking just how much of what we label as 'behavioural' is a dog's reaction to undiagnosed health issues.

Getting the Full Picture

When a dog bites, a lot goes into it. A dog's behaviour is a result of many components: their breed, history, current health and current environment. Consider the impact of breed traits. Some breeds are skittish by nature and startle easily, some guard easily, some breeds are more alert and some herd easily. If we put herding dogs near children who are running and screaming, the children might get nipped as the dogs follow their natural instinct and try to herd the children. If we put guarding dogs in the yard or on the terrace and leave them alone, they may take on the responsibility of guarding the premises. Such dogs will be on edge when people enter or leave. Sighthounds tend to be skittish and easily spooked. The things that stress or trigger dogs depend on their breeds. Knowledge of this helps us understand, to some extent, the behaviours of our dogs.

Then, there is the history of the individual dog. Their past experiences may have taught them that all humans are bad news or all dogs are bad news or a combination of that sort. It is not only rescue dogs or those from puppy mills that are at risk of being exposed to bad experiences and such bad lessons. Early imprinting happens so fast that it can happen to dogs in any situation—knowingly or unknowingly. Then there also seem to be the less understood mechanisms by which fear of the mother gets passed down to the puppies.

The genetics and history of the dog, however, do not complete the picture. For example, not all Rottweilers bite when you cross their territory, not all German Shepherds herd and not all rescue dogs are fearful. The dog's present—their health and environment—also contribute significantly. Some part of my work involves exploring the past of the dog and recognizing breed traits that help me understand the dog. Those are factors I cannot change. But the biggest part of my job is to work with the dog's present, to identify what is currently going wrong inside the dog's body as well as outside, including their environment, and to see what can be changed to prevent things from getting worse and to make the dog feel better.

Need to Observe

Health is a huge part of the dog's present, but several health issues have subtle or no indicators and can be easily missed. There will be no limping, howling in pain, profuse bleeding, vomiting, pooping of blood or any such dramatic clinical symptoms. Many of these conditions are not always tested for, because the symptoms are too subtle for one to even notice or recognize. Even if something is suspected, it cannot always be confirmed—some conditions have no tests, some tests are not available for dogs, and some tests are not available in India.

Hypothyroidism is one example that is notorious for masquerading as a behavioural issue well before it becomes clinically diagnosable. It gets even more challenging due to the lack of right tests in India. Other conditions that go unnoticed frequently are digestive ones. Common digestive conditions that plague our dogs are malabsorption diseases, dietary intolerances and ulcers. Malabsorption diseases are diseases where the body, for some reason, is unable to absorb enough nutrition from the food that is provided. Consequently, the body continues to remain unsatiated and hungry. Now think about a dog that has been feeling hungry for a very long time. It should come as no surprise at all that these dogs also start presenting behavioural problems because they are highly irritable. They can rip things up, dig things, bark profusely and even bite. EPI, IBS, IBD, Sibo and Pancreatitis fall in this bracket and are notorious for sneaking up on people with no visible dramatic signs. Stomach ulcers are similar and known to also be associated with 'oral stereotypies' such as excessive licking and chewing. Dietary intolerances are notorious for being sneaky. They are somewhat like allergies, but not as dramatic in how they present. When I see a dog that is intolerant to wheat, gluten or lactose, I don't always see extreme reactions like we see in humans who have peanut allergies. You don't see a dog going into an anaphylactic shock. However, what you do see is that the overall health of the dog is not good. The coat could be poor; the digestion could be poor in general; or the dog could be irritable, hyperactive or lethargic.

The point is that a lot could be happening with a dog's health, and we unfortunately only notice issues once they become quite serious. It's very difficult to suspect discomfort in a seemingly happy dog, whose only fault is slightly hyperactive behaviour. It's tempting to dismiss that there might be any discomfort. The problem, however, is that our dogs are acting against themselves by hiding discomfort, and if we don't learn to get really good at looking for signs, the issue could get worse to a point where they end up biting. In this next essay, I give you some advice on how to track your dog's health and wellness. Additionally, in our website (www. dogknowsbook.com), I have included books that can help pet parents understand how to track a dog's health. There is one book dedicated to understanding canine hypothyroidism, due to its high occurrence among our pet dogs. And of course, there are books by Julia—to help you understand chronic pain issues, which start very early in life.

SAUMFARING

Saumfaring is Turid's idea. It's a Norwegian concept that translates to 'investigation through observation and study'. Simply put, it's a few minutes spent to thoroughly—visually and tactically—examine our dogs with the deliberate intent of identifying key indicators of discomfort or poor health. When examining a dog, try to notice the following:

- Coat patterning and any changes in these patterns
- Oily and dry patches on the coat
- Skin condition
- Odour of the skin and dandruff
- Hot and cold areas
- Reaction to touch on different parts of the body
- Bumps, wounds, calluses, warts and other irregularities on the body
- The condition of the eyes, ears, teeth (odours, change in colour and any discharge)
- Dry snout or any discharge. Dryness may be an indication of pain in the neck and discharge might be a sign of allergies or an infection.
- Notice musculature, if there are any muscles that seem overly developed while others seem

underdeveloped or too soft. Do you find the neck very thick or the shoulders very bulky relative to other body parts of the dog? These could be indicators of certain muscles overcompensating for other muscles that are unable to function well.

Movement

Apart from performing saumfaring on your dog, it's a good idea to spend a few minutes to observe how they move. If they are experiencing discomfort in a certain area, they often alter their gait to compensate for it, even if only slightly. This can provide valuable clues as to what a dog might be feeling, so pay close attention to their movement. Here are some tips on how to do so:

- Notice how they walk or run. Watch out specifically for any limping, swaying of the hip, bunny-hopping while running, stiff or hyperflexible joints. These movements could be an indication that a dog is trying to protect certain joints. A myotherapy expert would be able to further analyse which joints are being protected by the dog and how to proceed with the situation at hand.

- Some dogs have a funny way of sitting, which makes for popular Internet memes, but we should analyse that. Are they sitting on their butt? Are their legs to one side or spread out in the front?

They might be sitting in these positions because they do not intend to use the hind legs to propel themselves while getting up. Or perhaps they are unable to bend their knees and/or hips in a certain way.

- When dogs are navigating stairs, pay close attention to how they are doing so. Are they hesitating to climb up or come down? This might indicate stiff shoulders or pain in the hips or knees. Are they tumbling down, suggesting that they have no control over the hind legs?

- Is the dog reluctant to sit or get up? Are the movements slow or deliberate? Make sure to make note of these points when heading to a health expert.

- Also make note of any sudden change in the nature of movement. For example, a stomach pain may manifest as an acute arch in the back or tucking in of the tummy.

While sudden change in movement is important and easier to notice, slow change in movement is equally important but more difficult to notice. If dogs are progressively changing the way they walk or sit, it might mean that progressive damage is taking place in certain parts of the body. The best way to identify this is to compare photographs and video footage taken a few months or even a few years back.

Behaviour

Behavioural indicators are the trickiest to observe. Few people associate strange behaviours with actual health issues. However, some of these may be the earliest indicators of discomfort in a dog and should be taken into account.

- **Hyperactivity** is often misunderstood. It can be a strong indicator of high levels of adrenaline and/or cortisol in the body as discussed in the essay on the topic. High levels of adrenaline and/ or cortisol could be the result of a dog needing to mask its pain, especially muscle pain. It is something I notice quite frequently among my clients' dogs that have joint or muscle issues trying to keep up with their humans. These dogs usually end up being hyperactive.

- **Mood alteration** is a common result of pain and discomfort. If the discomfort is sustained over a long period of time, the mood of a dog will be affected. Such dogs could be frequently in a **bad mood** and can get irritated quite easily. It is also understandable how such animals are more likely to snap, which manifests itself as aggression.

- **Lack of curiosity and excitement** can also be a manifestation of discomfort. However, quite often, the more passive behaviours are wrongly interpreted as obedience or calmness in a dog. This can be dangerous because in such cases, if the dog suddenly snaps and resorts to aggression, it can surprise or even scare people. Hypothyroidism is one of those conditions that tends to manifest itself in this way: dogs not only end up biting, but very quickly seem to forget the incident, almost as if they were in a trance.

For timely detection of underlying health issues with dogs, it is important to keep a close note of these instances and surrounding environmental factors, no matter how unrelated they may seem. In addition to extreme behaviours, it is important to look out for more subtle behavioural changes and keep track of any odd behaviours. These could include:

- **Chewing of the paw**: Muscular pain in the neck and shoulders can manifest as discomfort in the paws. The damage caused by collars can also result in a tingling sensation in the paws. Dogs might react to these sensations by licking their paws. Some dogs that have either arthritis in the hind legs or hip dysplasia may experience stiffness in the hind legs and tend to the react to the discomfort by chewing on their rump. Dogs with problems in the hind legs could also lick or chew their front legs, since those are under increased load from overcompensating for the lack of use of the hind leg.

- **Chasing of the tail**: Dogs chasing their tails is often seen as cute or funny, but in fact, can be another indicator of either physical discomfort in the rear part of the body or neurological discomfort. Lack of stability in the hips often causes the soft tissue called 'fascia' to get very tight near the rump area, right around the tail. Similarly, spinal issues can cause discomfort around the tail area. Dogs may try to deal with this by chasing the tail, rolling on their back or rubbing their rump against furniture or asking us to massage the area.
- **Shaking of the head**: This could be an indication of a headache, an issue with the ear(s), the sinuses or the tongue bone.
- **Stereotypies** such as digging, pacing and destruction.
- **Odd vocalizations** such as whimpering or howling.

Unfortunately, we lead very busy lives and are not always good at recognizing small details or identifying patterns in our dogs' behaviour, psychology and body. Memory has a strange way of consolidating itself, so we do not always store the frequency of events. Therefore, we cannot rely on our memory to reveal patterns to us. That is why it is critical that we keep a physical record by writing things down. Here are my recommendations on the most important things to record in your journal:

1. Any and all findings from the saumfaring
2. All mood changes, both good and bad
3. Poop and pee abnormalities in terms of the frequency, the quantity, texture, colour and any unusual odours emitting from waste matter
4. Any change in diet, appetite or water consumption
5. Any significant events in the entire household, even if they do not seem directly related to the dog. For example, loud noises emitting from a factory, a hotel or a flight path near your house
6. Any sudden changes in any of the above—newly developed habits, sudden aggression, sudden vocalization, sudden change in poop consistency.

Learning to Learn from Dogs

I don't believe any of us can claim to know everything there is to know about dogs. We don't always know what is good for them and often get things wrong. We get things wrong with ourselves too. Science gets it wrong too, often going back and forth between what is good and what is bad for humans. If we are going to get things wrong about ourselves, we are definitely going to get things wrong about our dogs. While this is easy to understand and admit, what is not is that dogs often get a lot of things right about themselves. Most people are unwilling to accept that dogs can understand some things about themselves better than we do.

What we seem to forget is that animals are very intuitive. Consider the concept of Zoopharmacognosy, which I discussed in the very first essay in this book. The idea behind it is that animals seem to have some intuitive ability not just to differentiate between what is toxic for them and what is not, but also what may have medicinal benefits for them. Then there is Galen Myotherapy, the idea of allowing the dog to guide the myofascial treatment. There is also the whole process by which dogs deal with their fear or learn to socialize with each other. These concepts have made me realize that dogs understand more than we give them credit for. The thing about this school of thought is that once you subscribe to it and start looking for what dogs know, you are entering a whole new world. It seems that our dogs know a lot, communicate a lot, have complex social interactions and are far more interesting than humans tend to think.

With all this in mind, I set up BHARCS, a school that aims to enable people to learn about dogs—but from dogs themselves, rather than relying on human opinion. Our motto is 'Learning to Learn from Dogs', and our aim is to try to become better 'listeners'.

CHAPTER 9

TALKING TO ANIMALS

We know that many animals in nature communicate with each other—whales, dolphins, elephants, chimpanzees. We know that wolves are master communicators. With dogs, however, we seem less inclined to observe and look for any kind of a language they might share. We are more inclined to teaching them how to understand our commands. I don't recall watching a single video of Dr Jane Goodall yelling commands in English to the chimpanzees. I cannot imagine ethologists attempting it with any other free-ranging animal—a tiger, an elephant or wolves (apart from in circuses). But when it comes to dogs, there seems to be very little interest in observing them and a lot more interest in training and commanding them. The bulk of literature we find on pet dogs deals with issues about teaching them our ways and how to make them understand us, not learning to observe them and reading *their* language.

It should not be too hard, should it? My grandfather seemed to communicate rather easily with them, with no need for him to teach them commands in his language. He did not seem to need science to know what his dogs felt and what the appropriate response would be. He was wise in recognizing fear in dogs and taught us to always back away from fearful animals. He dealt with the emotions of animals with due respect. He did not need a textbook to classify a growl as a 'distance-creating signal'. He intuitively understood that if any animal was growling, the right thing to do was to slowly back away them. In turn, the dogs that he adopted knew how to follow him to the field and when to go back home with him. They knew when not to cross boundaries that were set by him. The more I learn about Turid's way, the more I realize that she is getting us to understand how to recreate this ancient relationship that exists between humans and dogs. It also got me wondering why I needed a Turid to teach me this, while my grandfather seemed to have known all along. Are we losing our instincts and skills with our fellow animals? Is it perhaps because we are not spending as much time around animals? Our city lives take us very far from nature. Is this the price we are paying for this distance that we have created?

Redefining Our Relationship with Our Dogs

Turid challenged my right to be obeyed by my dogs. After having done enough soul-searching, I accepted the challenge and gave up that expectation, which meant that I could not command them and had to find another way to maintain harmony with them. I had to learn to ask and negotiate.

Negotiations are built on win-win situations, which can be arrived at if we know what a dog values. Dogs do value things beyond food, sometimes in far more meaningful ways than they cherish food. It could be the sense of control over their own lives, freedom from fear, newly acquired skills, a problem well solved or a fantastic new odour that brings with it a flurry of social information.

Consider what we are asking of our dogs when we get them to heel obediently on walks. They are yanked away if they try to stop to sniff something or to signal to another dog passing by. These dogs are home all day, and their only exposure to the outside world is through these short walks. Even during these, they are not being allowed to be curious about the world that they live in. Should curiosity not be a fundamental right? All other free animals get to be curious, and we never demand that they give their curiosity up. Don't our dogs deserve what other animals take for granted?

The reality of living in our homes is that irrespective of how much we provide for them, we have to set a few boundaries. These, however, can be kept to a minimum and drawn in a way that is mindful of a dog's right to choice and the dog's needs. Consider a dog that is jumping on people and needs to be asked to stop. If I believed the dog had no right to freedom, then I may simply command the dog to sit, like I used to ask Nishi. In contrast, if I believe in giving the dog a choice, then my boundary is limited to not wanting the dog to jump on me. The dog could choose to sit, stand, walk around, lie down, pick something up in the mouth or even walk away. I now focus only on telling my dogs that I don't like getting jumped on. As long as they don't jump on me, I have no expectations of how they are supposed to greet me. That is up to each dog. Cheerwal likes to lick my fingertips. Nishi likes to rub against my legs like a cat and then wants me to sit down so she can sit on my lap. Both work fine for me, and neither requires my dogs to obey me.

When I was learning how to convey to dogs that I didn't like being jumped on, as I mentioned earlier, I tried to practise on my father's dog, Puma. I did not command him to do anything specific. I just communicated to him that I did not appreciate him jumping on me, but he was free to do anything else. What Puma chose to do instead of jumping on me was quite surprising and gleeful. He found it difficult not to jump when he was excited, but he did understand and respect that I did not like being jumped on. He found the perfect solution that worked for both of us. He'd run a few feet away from me, jump up and down like he was on a trampoline, then come running up to me to get himself petted for a few seconds. He would repeat this a few times. Puma's brother, Buttons, would pick up something in his mouth and run around a bit. The entire scene is adorable.

This is where the right to freedom of choice makes a difference. If I had given them a command, like asking them to sit, can you imagine what a disaster it would have been for both these dogs? A command is not flexible, it is final. It is not tailored for the individual that I am trying to work with. A command is decided by one person and is not necessarily the best option for both parties. The best option is often determined by both parties working on it together. A win-

win solution is dynamic in nature. It is not a single cookie-cutter solution that one side comes up with. It depends on the situation, the individuals, and their current motivation. Identifying the perfect win-win situation requires good communication. I have discovered that learning to read and talk to dogs has helped me immensely in offering that freedom of choice to them. I love the effect it has had on my dogs.

Turid talks about this extensively, because choices do wonders for the brain, whereas lack of choices is more damaging than we understand. Julia talks of choices as well, insisting that the reason she is so successful in delivering her treatment to dogs is because it is treatment by choice. The last essay of this chapter is dedicated to my mentors and discusses choices.

CHOICES

'Choices, choices, choices!'
—Turid Rugaas

When we were in class, I would often hear Turid go on and on about choices. At first, I wondered what the big deal was. It's not like any of us kept our animals in terrible conditions, completely deprived of freedom. Moreover, how was giving choices going to be a solution for problem behaviours in dogs? However, I decided to take a deeper look into the subject because of Turid's insistence on how critical choices are.

I decided to start by examining what is really important to our animals and how much control pet dogs have over things that they value the most. When I compiled the list, it absolutely shocked me. It seemed that pet dogs had basically been asked to give up choice in almost every aspect of their lives that mattered to them. I had always known that giving up choices was a price we were asking our dogs to pay in exchange for luxury, but it was only now that I was beginning to understand the magnitude of this price.

In his book, *Why Zebras Don't Get Ulcers*, Dr Robert Sapolsky discusses at length the impact of predictability and choice on stress. The subject seems rather well-researched with both rats and humans. The simplest of the studies seems to be the one done on rats, where it was shown that even enjoyable things like running on the wheel stopped being enjoyable and became very stressful when the rats did not have a choice of when to get on and off the wheel. Studies on humans showed that jobs that gave people very little control over what they did were far more stressful than having a job with massive responsibility or a deadline. Therefore, it is understandable that when on a walk, if a dog is acting unpredictably, the person can feel a loss of a sense of control, which may stress them out immensely. Unfortunately, most people react to this by trying to bring back a sense of control at the expense of the dogs losing their sense of control over the situation. This is a zero-sum game, and eventually, one of the two will become stressed, which will also stress the other out. This is a vicious cycle.

The question this discussion brings us to is whether there are practical ways to reintroduce choice into our dogs' lives without putting them at risk and without having to feel a loss of control ourselves. The good news is that there are, and better yet, dogs don't always need true choices. Several studies on rats and humans confirm that just the semblance of choice also works, that as long as we believe that we are in control, we are less likely to get stressed. My students and I have brainstormed a few ideas that I present to you here in each area that pet dogs are usually deprived of substantial control.

Food

Observation: Most pet dogs don't really get a say in what or when they are being fed. Today, we are aware that there is no one specific diet that is right for a dog and that nutritional needs vary based on age, breed, environment, current health and stress levels. However, most of our dogs are on a diet that is decided by us, not based on their ever-changing needs, but based on our beliefs or on what we are told is best for them. Dogs are put on this diet, which is repeated day after day. It's not until dogs start refusing to eat any food and end up starving for a few days that we take notice and make changes to their diet. More subtle signs are often ignored, sometimes even reprimanded.

Recommendation: While it may not always be possible to provide our dogs with a varied menu, it is possible to give them choices regarding flavours, in terms of herbs, oils or sauces. Some of my students prepare two different kinds of meals for their dogs and offer them a choice in the morning. The one the dog does not choose to eat is left aside to become their dinner. This way, no food is wasted. I grow different types of medicinal herbs in my garden. I give my dogs access to that part of the garden to graze in and supplement their food with the necessary herbs on their own.

While my dogs are on a fixed feeding schedule, I do let them decide if they want to eat a few miuntes early or late. I gladly meet their need if they feel peckish and want some snacks. But if their appetite changes dramatically, where they are insatiable or simply disinterested in food, then I will launch an investigation into the matter, while I continue to meet their need and feed them when they feel hunger.

Elimination

Observation: An unfortunate outcome of living indoors is that dogs don't have free access to the outdoors, where they can pee when they need to. Most dogs have to wait for their walks, which are done on schedule and a limited number of times. This means that several dogs not only fail to have the option of peeing when they need to but must also stick to human schedules. There is a misconception that dogs only need to poop once a day and pee twice a day. When we did a 'pee study' during our sessions with Turid, examining how many times a dog would pee given the choice, we noticed that many dogs do need to pee several times a day, just like humans. It varies based on weather, health of the dog, age, sex of the dog and environmental stressors.

Recommendation: I feel that it should be mandatory for all of us to provide our dogs with the option to pee when they need to. Holding in pee longer than they should not only feels terrible but can also lead to kidney problems. What I typically recommend for clients in India is to try giving a dog a spot on their terrace or balcony and allow the sun to deal with the smell. Some clients prefer to give their dogs access to one of the bathrooms. One way or the other, we must figure out a way, irrespective of how limited space is. It is important for us to try and make some space for our dogs to be able to pee and poop when they need to because it is a basic biological function and is as important as access to drinking water or food.

Sleep

Observation: Some dogs are not given a choice of the surfaces and places they sleep in. Dogs who are typically kept in kennels or crates lose choice in this matter. Here, too, dogs prefer different surfaces based on a host of factors such as temperature, health, condition of joints and time of day. The essay on sleep talks about how not having a choice in this matter can negatively impact sleep quality and how that, in turn, can lead not only to behavioural issues but also to compromises in the dog's physical and mental health and well-being.

Recommendation: Some rules become necessary in most households, such as dogs not being allowed on beds, for various reasons like allergies or space constraints. I tell my clients to define those boundaries very well, but to give free access to their dogs when it comes to the rest of the space in the house, to allow them to exert some choice. Sometimes, it might be necessary to puppy-proof the house or set up a puppy-proofed area for a certain period of time until the dogs learn to take care of themselves and remain safe inside the house. However, the dogs can be given a semblance of choice even in this situation by giving them multiple beds/surfaces to sleep on and freedom of movement.

Walks

Observation: Most dogs do not really have much choice on any aspect of a walk. The timings of when the walks take place are almost always dictated by pressing human calendars. The equipment is chosen by the people, and most times, the duration, route and pace are also chosen by people. Some dogs are denied the choice of how close or far they would like to walk from people. In some extreme situations, I have even seen dogs deprived of the option of stopping to sniff or even look around.

Recommendation: It is hard to give dogs control when it comes to some aspects of a walk. Typically, the timing of a walk is dictated by our calendars. However, there are other aspects over which a dog can be given a great deal of control. I like the idea of having multiple walking equipment and offering my dog a choice on the kind of walking equipment they'd like to use. One can also try and give the dogs control over where they walk or which route they take. However, there might be unsafe areas that we want to protect them from. For example, I do not like to walk my dogs on busy streets because I feel it is unsafe for them. So we have identified a few neighbouring routes and grounds we deem safe. When we take them to these places, my dogs decide the direction they would like to move in as well as the pace. It's very easy to give dogs a choice of what they want to sniff or watch and how long they want to do it, limiting them only when it's dangerous. In India, it's not uncommon to encounter garbage that might contain poisoned food. So when I see a garbage pile, I steer clear of it, walking in a wide arc around it. Other than this, the girls decide what they want to sniff or explore. While the upper limit as to how long these walks can be is determined by my calendar, I do factor in a certain degree of flexibility into that timing, so that if the girls want to start or end the walk ten to fifteen minutes sooner, they have the option to do so.

Social contact

Observation: Almost all parts of this are often determined by humans. The people and dogs that our dog gets to meet are entirely under our control. We decide when they need to meet others, where they meet them, and how many dogs and people they need to deal with at any given point in time. Some dogs might reclaim their choice by expressing dislike for a person or a dog. This is not considered acceptable behaviour, and the dog is often sent into behaviour correction training.

Recommendation: Obviously, we cannot have our dogs walking out whenever they want. But we can try and tune into the kinds of dogs and people they want to meet and those they want to avoid. We can give them access to the kind of social contact they are comfortable with. To be able to read this carefully, it is important to note that one-on-one social interactions with people and dogs is much better than group interactions, because reading subtle dog body language is an art, and it takes time for us to be able to understand and react appropriately to it.

Leisure

Observation: Dogs have evolved to somewhat work with our schedules, so they tend to be active for a few hours during the morning and for a few hours during the evening. This makes it easier for us to engage with our dogs when they most likely want it. However, the exact timing, the type of engagement and how long we want to engage with them are mostly determined by human beings, based on their beliefs of what they think their dog needs. A lot of the decisions are based on the human's calendar, energy levels and efforts required. For example, I have sometimes had clients not allowing dogs to roll on the grass, worried about the effort involved in washing the dogs.

Recommendation: Here too, there is a certain constraint with how long we can engage with our dogs and during what time. With my dogs, I try to introduce choice in how I engage with them. I usually offer them a choice of puzzles, stories and search games that allow them to choose the way in which they want to engage. The girls have developed their unique ways of responding to, 'What do you want to do now, puppy?'

The notion of having a life that is somewhat under your own control increases confidence and decreases stress. This is easy to see in dramatic situations where animals are rescued from abusive confinement. As they begin to gain some degree of control with their movements, their confidence, well-being and happiness improve drastically. Moreover, a sense of control also makes enjoyable things feel better. Studies on both pigeons and rats seem to suggest that while being given food obviously brought them joy, allowing them to determine when they get that food brought them much more joy. In effect, increased control increases joy and reduces stress, which in turn can reduce problem behaviours that are a direct result of chronic stress. Sometimes, these things can almost feel like a magical panacea that has unrelated but desirable consequences.

The psychological impact of the extreme loss of choice is a condition called 'learnt helplessness'. This is a state in which individuals inaccurately feel inadequate to cope with the situation they face, because past experiences have shown them that they don't have any control. In other words, it's a state of having given up. Learnt helplessness in humans is known to be one of the causes of depression and other mental illnesses. In the 1960s and 1970s, psychologists studied this condition in dogs through the use of some rather unpleasant experiments. Several dogs were made to experience unpleasantness that they could neither predict nor control, for prolonged periods of time. Later, when control was reintroduced into their environment and the dogs had the opportunity to escape the unpleasantness, they continued to stay and experience the unpleasantness, having either forgotten how to escape or given up. Unfortunately, learnt helplessness can often look like obedience and can also quite easily afflict our dogs if we are not able to see that a certain experience is causing unpleasantness.

An example of this is when Uttam and I were observing a dog being walked in a busy railway station in Europe. The dog was tiny, and all the noise, sounds and movement around were clearly terrifying. However, the lady walking him was busy trying to figure out which platform she wanted to go to by looking at the schedule on her phone and was also pulling along with her a large suitcase. The dog was terrified of not only the people but also the suitcase. He had no idea what the plan was and how to escape all the commotion. As we continued to watch the dog, he gradually started shutting out the environment around him, stuck his snout behind the lady's legs and just blindly followed her. What is most unfortunate is that I have heard this state of mind being labelled as 'obedience' and 'good behaviour'.

This quality of learnt helplessness to shut an animal down and have their behaviour resemble obedience is also something that is inadvertently used in certain training techniques. Flooding, for example, is a classic case of inducing learnt helplessness to mask fearful behaviour. I was once talking to a trainer who was dealing with a dog who had a fear of people and had therefore started to bite people. He decided to resolve this by walking the dog on a short leash and a choke chain and taking him to a market where there would be a lot of people present. He then showed me a video of the dog being unreactive despite being crowded by a group of children, claiming that the dog had been fully 'cured of his aggressiveness'. This was a very unfortunate situation where the dog had entirely shut down, but from the perspective of the trainer and other human beings, it seemed that the problem had been solved. Attempting to solve problems this way poses huge risks. When the little dog that was considered 'cured of the aggression' returned home, he started biting again.

It was then attributed to the people in the house not knowing how to control the dog. What really happened was that the learnt helplessness started to fade when the dog came back home, perhaps due to a significant reduction in his stress levels. This led to him beginning to express his fears and emotions again. Unfortunately, due to the 'flooding' exercise, the underlying fear had worsened, making the biting much worse. Apart from its ineffectiveness as a long-term solution, learnt helplessness is also heartbreaking to witness when we understand what it really means for a dog.

I will end this section with an example of Bozo's human, one of my favourite clients. When Bozo had just arrived in his new home, he had been through severe trauma and was biting people. At the same time, he was also severely unwell and needed to be medically examined. Therefore, Bozo's humans had felt that they had no choice but to muzzle him for the examination. As Bozo's mum narrated this story to me, tears welled up in her eyes. She said, 'It was heartbreaking to see how he knew exactly what a muzzle was. The second we put it on him, he immediately lay down, completely still and let us do to him whatever it was that we wanted to do. It was very clear that he had been put in situations before where, when the muzzle came on, any option to do what he wanted was taken away from him. That's when I decided he will never have to go back to that state of mind again, and I would not like to use a muzzle. Please help me out.'

Only after such close examination of the topic of choices did it occur to me how something this subtle and seemingly unimportant can hugely impact a dog's physical and mental well-being. The worst part about loss of choices and control is that the outcome often resembles a calm or obedient dog. In addition, because our senses are not as keen as that of a dog's, and because we have a better understanding of the world we have created and live in, the environment around us is not as overwhelming to us. Therefore, it can be hard for us to understand the things that can stress out a dog. Given this and our frequent ineptitude when it comes to reading subtle stress signs, it is very easy for us to unwittingly put our dogs in situations that can overwhelm them. I can now see where Turid's mantra 'choices, choices, choices' comes from.

For the Love of the Planet

This philosophy of respecting the choices of individuals is quite powerful and is applicable far beyond just dogs. It is applicable to all aspects of life and has far-reaching consequences. Given the world we are faced with today, how valuable would it be if all our children grow up with the understanding that when they are dealing with someone more vulnerable than them, they must never resort to stripping that individual of their choices. To me, my journey with dogs has been more than just about dogs. It has changed the way I interact with animals. It has changed the way I look at people, and it has deepened my understanding of my own behaviour and instincts. It has brought me peace and given my life meaning.

One of my students, who had recently become a mum, said to me, 'Sindhoor, I must tell you that your philosophy with dogs inspired how I am bringing up my child. I am a lot more patient. In general, it has made me a more pleasant person with other people too.' Of course, at that point, I did feel very overwhelmed by what she said to me and thanked her for sharing such kind words. When I thought about it later, I realized that it should not really be surprising. What I teach my students and what I learnt from my teachers is the idea of empathy towards another species. Once you get that, it is hard not to be empathetic to our own species.

My students and clients sometimes break down during our sessions. I think a lot about why that happens. Let me see if I can paint you a picture. Remember that iconic Jane Goodall picture where she is extending her finger to touch a baby chimpanzee's finger? You have perhaps experienced that tingling feeling just by imagining what that touch might have felt like. I used to be a diver, and once, a turtle swam by me. As he did, he came straight up to me, touched my mask, and then swam away. In that moment, I felt that very tingling sensation. My students feel it too. It's the feeling my clients get when they use body language to say something to their dogs, and their dogs understand it and return a signal that the client recognizes. This feeling is unique, is it not? You too must have felt it when a butterfly lands on your finger or a scared animal gains courage to approach you. You may even have felt it just by looking at a big cat or an elephant or a wolf and felt so overwhelmed by their beauty that you've wanted to preserve them, not necessarily for what they do for mankind but simply because something so beautiful needs to be preserved. This, in my mind, is love.

I see love as nature's masterpiece. It makes us want to put the object of our love above all else and to protect it with our life. Conservation and rescue can often be a result of such love. The unfortunate side-effect of urbanization is that we have been cut off from animals and nature. It seems that we are paying a heavy price for this in the form of apathy towards not only animals but also the planet in general. Yet, despite shrunken urban dwellings, tightening schedules, reduced time for our loved ones and crunching resources, our love for dogs seems to continue to make us bring animals into our homes. So, could we perhaps begin to look at them as ambassadors of the rest of the animal kingdom, as something that might open our communication channels with the rest of the animal world?

Turid starts off her classes with a quote from Chief Dan George, which I think is a good way to say goodbye to you wonderful folk, who, like me, have felt the spark when you've made a special connection with an animal. That is perhaps the connection that will save this planet. Value it and nurture it. Connect with animals.

'If you talk to the animals they will talk with you and you will know each other. If you do not talk to them you will not know them, and what you do not know you will fear. What one fears, one destroys.'

ACKNOWLEDGEMENTS

This book took me five years to write and involved many individuals contributing with support, research, knowledge and inspiration. There are many people and dogs I would like to express my gratitude towards. I would like to start by thanking all the dogs that have patiently stood by me, waiting for me to figure out my relationship with animals. Of course, Nishi and Cheeru are at the forefront of this journey. But I must also mention the countless other dogs, including Jeanu, Denny, Puma, Buttons, Sunny, Blacky, Snowy, Bozo, Mishka, Sesi, Pops, Kajal, Kermit, Crowly, Poppy, Red, Flashy, the dogs of my clients, students and, of course, all the street dogs of Bangalore, whom I have the continued privilege of interacting with and learning from.

I must also thank my mentors, Turid Rugaas and Julia Robertson, who have not only been instrumental in defining the course of my journey but have also had infinite amount of patience with all my questions and have always been just a call or email away.

About halfway through writing the fourth version of this book, my wrists gave way and Aisvarya Subramaniam came to my rescue, transcribing chapter after chapter. Sangeetha Jayakaran, one of my oldest students, stepped up and did the necessary research for the book. This book would never have happened without their selfless and reliable help.

I must express my gratitude to my parents for instilling the love of animals and the love of science in me; to my sister for being my biggest cheerleader; to Agnes and Anne Lill Kvam for hosting me in Norway and giving me the chance to embark on this journey; to Grace Shen and Elizabeth Mckeon, who made my education in the US possible; to Suman Bolar for taking me in when I had nowhere to go; to Aprajitha Suryanarayanan and Sanjeev Nivedan, for reviewing the book early on and giving me the critical feedback; to Gargi Singh for the illustrations; and to my friends and students who stood by me through the toughest of times and continue to believe in me. There have been so many of you—please excuse me if I have not named each of you, but I know, in my heart, I am here because of you.

And last but not least, to my best friend and husband, Uttam. You believed in me when I did not. You heard what my heart desired when I could not hear it. You pushed me where I needed to go, even when I could not see it. You supported me in every way possible. And most of all, you are the best papa Nishi and Cheeru could ever have, which has filled my life with hope and strength. You and Nishi are no more in our world, but you will live on in my heart for ever, shining a light on my path as I journey through this world without you. Nishi, my sweet little girl, your spirit inspires me to walk this path with love and hope, regardless of the pain life throws at me. Uttam, my darling, the lessons I learnt with you and from you provide me the wisdom I need, to know right from wrong. While doing the right thing at all times is not going to be easy in the face of pain, my dear Nishi and Uttam, your love gives me the strength and courage to stay the course. I miss you so much and so do the countless lives you touched with your kindness and love. We will keep the light burning bright.

ABOUT THE AUTHOR

Sindhoor Pangal is an engineer-turned-canine behaviour consultant and canine myotherapist. After her dog Nishi met with an accident, requiring special physical and emotional care, Sindhoor quit her corporate life as vice president of a Silicon Valley-based start-up to pursue a career working with dogs. After she started working as a behaviour and myotherapy consultant for companion dogs, she discovered her passion for ethological studies of free-ranging dogs in India. She is currently the principal and director of the Bangalore-based BHARCS, an academy that educates pet parents and professionals on canine behaviour and ethology. BHARCS offers a one-of-its kind, UK-accredited, Level-4 diploma on Canine Behaviour and Ethology. The institution attracts students from all over the world and has a distinguished set of students from over seven countries and fifteen cities in India. While she wears many hats, Sindhoor's favourite role has been being a mommy to two amazing dogs—Nishi, who recently passed away, and Cheeru—whom she considers her inspirations and her greatest teachers.

To see more pictures and videos of Nishi, Cheeru and the streeties of Bangalore, and to check out the complete list of references and recommended readings, visit www.dogknowsbook.com